What is exhibition design?

"Storytelling is the most powerful way to
put ideas into the world today."

Robert McAfee Brown

RotoVision

A RotoVision Book

Published and distributed by RotoVision SA
Route Suisse 9
CH-1295 Mies
Switzerland

RotoVision SA
Sales and Editorial Office
Sheridan House, 114 Western Road
Hove BN3 1DD, UK

Tel: +44 (0)1273 72 72 68
Fax: +44 (0)1273 72 72 69
www.rotovision.com

10 9 8 7 6 5 4 3 2 1

ISBN: 978-2-88893-127-0

Art Director: Tony Seddon
Design: JCLanaway

Reprographics in Singapore by ProVision Pte. Ltd.
Tel: +65 6334 7720
Fax: +65 6334 7721

Printed in China by Midas Printing International Ltd..

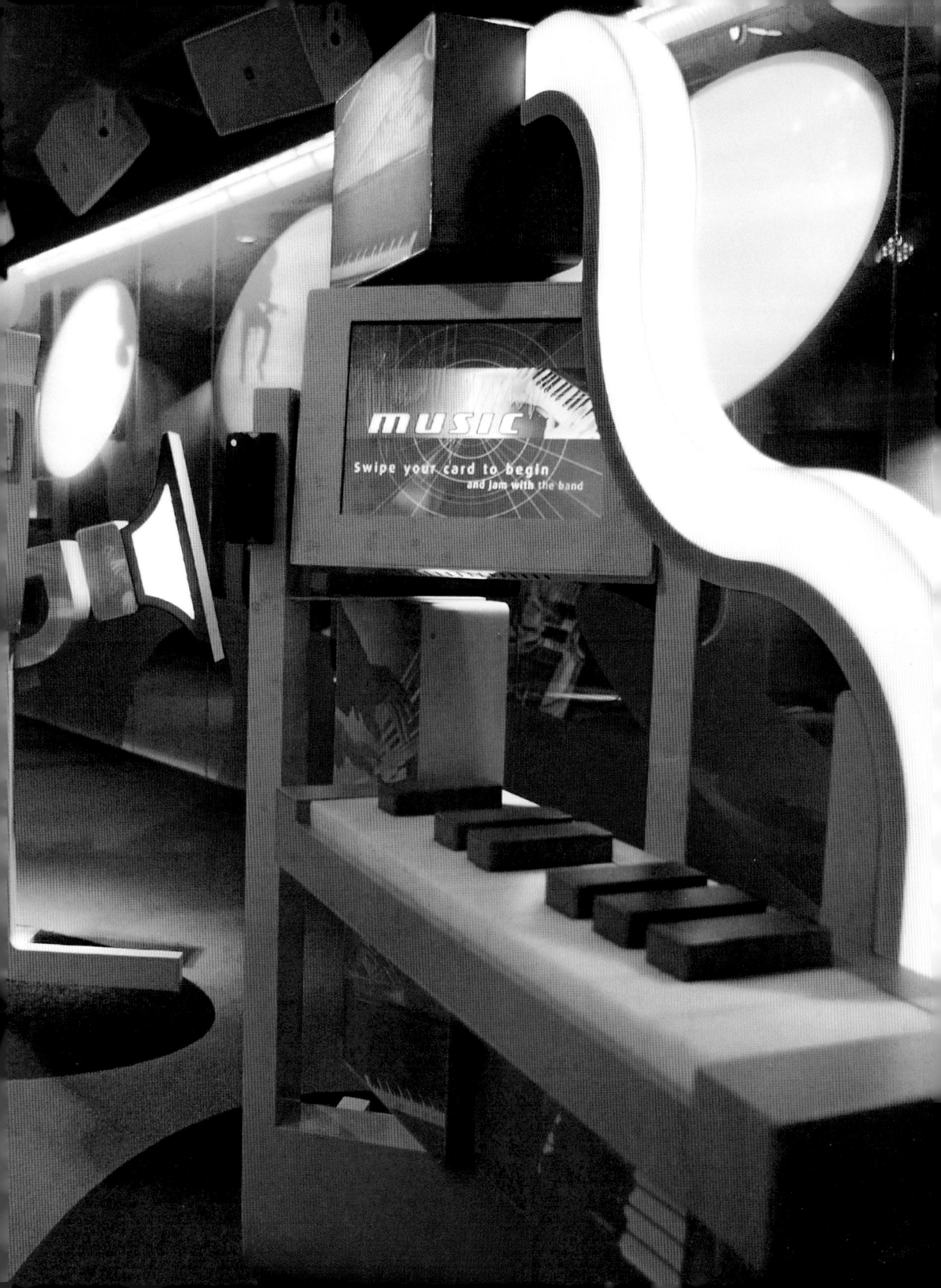
music
Swipe your card to begin
and jam with the band

Issues

Anatomy

Portfolios

Etcetera

Preface

When RotoVision approached the Society for Environmental Graphic Design (SEGD) with the idea about a book defining exhibition design, it opened up a number of debates and discussions inside the organization about the nature of exhibition design. Over the past few years, SEGD has been focusing on defining exhibition design as a merger of communication and environments. Defining it in this way opened the door to contributions by designers that at one time may have been called architects, curators, industrial designers, or historians, but by their design vision and ability to collaborate are creating a distinctly unique field. This definition brought up a number of debates and required careful treading among a variety of existing and entrenched fields. There are several organizations that already exist that specialize in museum exhibitions, trade shows, and heritage parks. Our premise that exhibition design has a process that is consistent across all these areas would require careful and consistent analysis. This book should be judged as much by what is excluded as what is included.

This book is not meant to be the last word on exhibition design, but to serve as a clear statement about the nature of what the authors and SEGD consider to be the direction exhibition design is developing in. The focus is on collaboration; the balancing of space, object, and information; the subtle integration of technology; and the role of the audience. All of these trends have made exhibition design the cutting edge field it is evolving into.

The chapters of this book explore the infinite variety of design firms that develop exhibitions, from industrial designers to interior designers to theatrical designers. All of the professional disciplines are different, but many of the skills and design processes required to produce the exhibitions are similar. They all require simultaneous engagement in both two-dimensional and three-dimensional design thinking, and must master the craft of storytelling in the environment.

Finally, this book is dedicated to illustrating the mastery of design craft in areas ranging from museums to trade shows in venues around the world. In a world envisioned in this way, designers will be known less by what their discipline is than by their vision and ability to collaborate in vast and complex ways, creating enjoyable and educational environments.

Jonathan Alger
Board President, SEGD

Leslie Gallery Dilworth
Executive Director, SEGD

What is exhibition design?

A tremendous amount of research has gone into uncovering exactly when humans first began to communicate and how that evolved into the myriad forms of communication we use today. One thing that is clear is that somewhere along the line—perhaps quite early on—people started using objects and the environment around them as tools in satisfying their instinctual impulse to expose, enlighten, celebrate, revere, sell, and interpret aspects of their experience. These "environments that communicate" can be seen as the precursors of a typology of human experience, as well as an increasingly recognized—if not well-defined—area of creative practice: exhibition design.

This book is organized around the recognition that there presently exists a broad and varied range of projects that constitute the realm of "exhibition," and that, for our discussion, the qualities they share are more important than the many ways in which they differ. Further, it must be noted that while we are at a point in our history where numerous professional and trade organizations, as well as institutions of higher education, are catering to and offering academic degrees in the field of exhibition design, the fact is that we would be hard pressed to call it a profession. It might be more accurate to characterize exhibition design as an integrative process, bringing together in varying degrees architecture, interior design, environmental graphic design, print graphics, electronics and digital media, lighting, audio, mechanical interactives, and other design disciplines. Nevertheless, it would be a mistake to deny its distinct identity or its impact. Much attention has been given to the power that environments have for imparting and interpreting information, involving audiences, and influencing understanding. And while we cast a large net over a wide range of projects in capturing this field of practice, it is what they have in common that defines them as a group.

From museum exhibitions, retail spaces, and trade shows to themed entertainments, information kiosks, visitor centers, World's Fairs, and expositions, exhibition design involves itself in creating experiences in real time, utilizing space, movement, and memory to facilitate multilayered communication. In whatever type of venue or situation their skills are engaged, exhibition designers work in multidisciplinary teams with their clients to help them tell their stories to their desired audience. They physically shape the experience, often acting in the role of composer, orchestrator, choreographer, and conductor, to ensure that the intended messages are delivered in the most compelling and meaningful way. They harness the powerful interpretive potential of space to deliver narratives to human beings, who are "hardwired" to receive messages through this medium. Melding communication design and the built environment, exhibition design creates environments that communicate.

Right: *Hollywood Shadow Project*
Designed by Cameron McNall. Nothing shows the blending of the barriers between storytelling, environmental design, exhibition design, and public art better than the *Hollywood Shadow Project*. The intention is to evoke memory, as it is constituted via photographs and movies, and present this memory on the site of its invention: Hollywood. All of the project sites incorporate buildings and businesses involved in making movies. It is also significant that the sculpture silhouettes were captured via optical means and then reprojected via the sun, which offers both light and motion. The installation leaves it to the audience to interpret the story. Is it a narrative of the past, a commentary on the present, an attempt to establish an identity for the future, or just a way of establishing a wonderful sense of space and place?

Below: Venn diagram
This diagram defines the blending of communication design and environmental design to create a fusion: environments that communicate. Exhibition design, environmental design, public art, and technology design all fall into this camp.

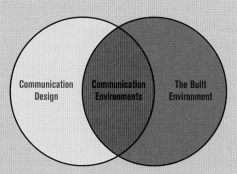

Figurine Empties,
URART Gallery
Designed by Burkhardt
Leitner constructiv, Akın
Nalça Tanıtım ve Tasarım
Hizmetleri Limited, and
Sabine Mescher-Leitner.
This exhibition at the URART
Gallery in Istanbul uses the
configuration of objects
in space to tell a story.

Left: *A Sign of Democracy,*
National Center for the
Preservation of Democracy
Designed by C&G Partners.
This flap sign displays
inspirational quotes, poems,
questions, and statements
about democracy. Unlike
normal flap signs, this one has
no labels or markings on it
other than the letters that
appear when the flaps move.
When it is blank, it is mute.
The spirit of democracy
comes alive in this piece,
which changes every so often
to a new quote or poem line
by line, letter by letter, in a
noisy cascade that can be
heard throughout the lobby.

I SWEAR TO THE LORD
I STILL CAN'T SEE
WHY DEMOCRACY MEANS
EVERYBODY BUT ME.

LANGSTON HUGHES

Immersive exhibitions
These exhibitions are
completely immersive
environments, capturing a
literal look and feel of a place,
and deepening the experience
with multiple interpretive areas.
Below right: *The Rock Island
Line: Building a Railroad,
Building a Dream*, The
Putman Museum. Designed
by Project Arts & Ideas.
Below left: *Capture of the
U505*, Chicago Museum of
Science and Industry.
Designed by Christopher
Chadbourne & Associates
with the Chicago Museum
of Science and Industry and
Edwards Technologies.

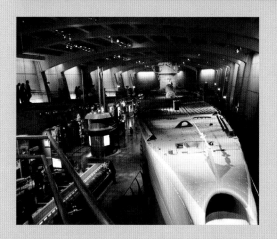

A brief history of exhibition design

There are two caveats one must accept when attempting to trace the history of exhibition design. The first is that, as with many phenomena, not to mention disciplines, pinpointing their beginnings in time or place is often quite difficult. Springing as they do from innate human urges and responses to external factors, they often present themselves in various cultures simultaneously and manifest themselves and develop at different rates. The second consideration lies in the fact that defining them can be tricky. They continue to evolve; they are slippery and hard to catch. In the case of exhibition design, we speak of a mode of communication that has meant different things at different times, continues to change and expand, and, in fact, is not even recognized universally as a discipline at all.

In scanning the history of exhibition design, it is nonetheless possible to note a few large-scale trends. For instance, that exhibitions have moved toward increased democratization. Once the exclusive province of the rich, the powerful, and the elitely educated, both access to and participation in the development of exhibitions has gradually come to include people at all levels of society. Another fascinating evolution has been the extreme broadening of the exhibition design vocabulary. From its beginnings in the static display of objects, we have seen forays into increased interpretation and didactic explanation, all forms of physical and electronic interactivity, multimedia presentations, architecture, theater, dance, performance art, and environmental graphics. And it is not by accident that we choose this point in time to assess and reflect upon the roots of exhibition design, for it has recently come fully into its own as a factor to be dealt with in the worlds of art, design, and communication. The public, as well as reviewers and commentators have begun to take notice of the important role that design plays in the character and success of visitor experiences of all kinds. Universities have responded by offering programs and degrees in exhibition design; professional and lay publications critique the quality of design; museums, retailers, trade organizations, and other public venues rely on exhibit and display design to further their aims and achieve their goals.

Cabinets of curiosities

Cabinets of curiosities emerged during the seventeenth century as people began to privately display and classify objects from all areas of the world that were considered to be exotic. Some of these exhibits were thought to represent models of the world, in that they contained as many specimens as possible. They were often organized and displayed in very unusual ways. Frequently composed as fully immersive environments, with objects seemingly arranged more for aesthetic effect than scientific explication, items were grouped together simply because of their color, or because they were all birds or flowers, or all the same shape. Some may call it an irrational organization but it was one that was based on a kind of primitive taxonomy. While taxonomy in the scientific realm was more concerned with classifying objects according to type or genre, species or origin, these miniature spectacles might appear to be specifically designed to create an astonishing presentation of grotesque oddities.

Francesco Calzolari's, Museum Calceolarium
Cabinets of curiosities were designed to display collections belonging to individuals. Francesco Calzolari's cabinet exhibited his natural history collection.

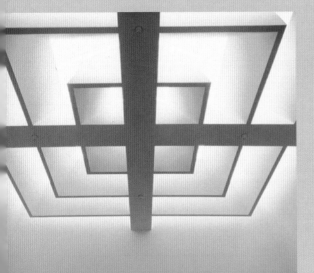

The Louvre Museum
The Louvre has been reorganized several times, most recently by **IM Pei** with Donovan and Green.

Palaces

While many royal palaces and historic houses have become publicly visited artifacts themselves, they have also frequently been converted into museums and art galleries. The Louvre Museum in Paris was originally built in the late twelfth century as a fortress, was then transformed into a palace for Charles V, and has been updated several times since. Early versions of the Louvre were akin to large warehouses, cramming as much into the space as possible. Even now, paintings in the larger, taller halls are stacked three high on top of each other. A recent renovation of the Louvre was mandated to, among other things, help reorganize reflection in a way that would make some historic and linear sense. The Hermitage in St. Petersburg, was built as the winter palace of Peter the Great in the early eighteenth century. With 1,050 rooms, it is now among the largest art museums in the world and can take weeks to appreciate in even a cursory way.

Church museums

For centuries, the Catholic Church had been collecting and bringing back to Rome artifacts, paintings, sculpture, mosaics, and religious icons from around the world. All around the city, storehouses filled with these objects were bursting at the seams. In the late eighteenth century the Church campaigned to create what is now known as The Vatican Museums. The Museums were designed in scale and purpose for specific types of display. There was an obvious interest in showing off objects in ways that elevated their level of grandeur so that each piece was seen as a great work of art or of great significance, reflecting the power and wealth of the Church. In large part, this was achieved through design, with niches, color, and architectural ornamentation lending the works tremendous impact as well as a sense of place and importance. It was an early example of "design as interpretation" being harnessed to contextualize and enhance the display of objects. The design was meant to interpret, celebrate, reveal, and enlighten.

The Capitoline Museum

The Capitoline Museum in Rome was built around 1734 and features artworks in a type of domestic setting. Arranged in the center of the room as well as the perimeter, these displays are less self-conscious than earlier attempts at similar presentations. The display of artifacts is somewhat random and haphazard, giving space to each object by putting them on pedestals, but certainly not interpreting them in any contextual or symbolic way.

The Capitoline Museum
Objects in this museum are placed on pedestals and arranged in a haphazard way.

Self-portrait of Charles Wilson Peale
This painting shows Peale pulling back the curtain to open up history and culture to a wider audience.

Charles Wilson Peale

Peale is credited with opening one of the first public museums in the US in 1786, which he called The Museum of Rational Entertainment. A model for the Smithsonian Institution in Washington, DC, his museum was to be the "nation's closet" or repository of all things worth saving and studying. Peale was among the first to take the collection out of the governmental, church, or royal gallery and present the museum as a place for collecting, preserving, and displaying culture. Whereas museums began as private venues for organizations and individuals who had the means to collect objects and display them, in a quite literal sense, Peale pulled back the curtain, exposing culture's history and treasures and inviting us all in.

Expositions

The exposition was an early stepping stone toward public museums and the idea of display for everyone. Beginning in the nineteenth century, these colossal events were similar to the cabinets of curiosities in that they consisted of found objects from exotic places. They differed, though, in how they also explicitly celebrated broader themes like faith, technology, and, above all, the driving force, spellbinding variety, and jaw-dropping spectacle of human progress. Objects were displayed on a huge scale, exoticism and familiarity vied for attention, and for the first time it was all accessible to the emerging middle and working classes. At the Paris World's Fair in 1900, large pavilions were purpose-built for specific exhibitions, though there was still the compulsion to present absolutely everything you could get your hands on that was deemed of importance without a thematic storyline orientation. Later, World's Fairs began to feature government and industry-sponsored pavilions, which were designed to deliver stories and iconography, not just for the display of precious objects. In this way, World's Fairs were precursors to themed entertainment parks and museums of science and industry.

Retail department stores

Early department stores, particularly in large cities, were not only purveyors of goods, but were also responsible for major advances in display and design communication. Often, items were displayed in thematic exhibitions without the direct intention of being sold, but rather to sell the store's overall brand— its power, reach, and sophistication, and of course to induce people to come and see the spectacle in the grand halls of the store. These exhibitions sought to display culture and elevate the store's brand in the eyes of consumers, through offering a kind of free, social entertainment.

Who do we design for?

It is impossible to communicate effectively if you don't who you're talking to. Your listener's personal history, cultural background, gender, age, abilities, and learning style have a tremendous impact on how the information you wish to share is received, processed, and understood. For this reason, when we set out to interpret a story through design, we start with defining our audience.

More than ever, exhibition environments are conceived of and utilized as places of intense social interaction. In fact, this group dynamic is one of the features that makes museums and other venues unique. Increasingly, mixed visitor groups are the norm. It is important to work with a client to determine the types of visitors they already attract, as well as those they want to bring in, if they are to reach them successfully through their exhibition. Do they tend to have older, more educated visitors? School groups? Families with children? Retired tourists? Do visitors come with significant foreknowledge of the subject, or will they consider the information alien and esoteric? Without a clear sense of some of these parameters, we might just as well be talking to the wall.

A little knowledge of your audience can go a long way. And the characteristics we seek to recognize will affect both cognitive and physical design. While older people with failing eyesight might appreciate brighter lighting and larger type on labels, teenagers conditioned to a life of video games and other interactive media will probably respond more favorably to environments full of visual and audio stimulation. Toddlers take in information tactilely, have short attention spans, and can be put off by spaces that are dark and dramatically lit. And, sadly, not only do most interpretive signs and labels go unread, but aiming the reading level too high is a sure recipe for confusion, even in exhibitions designed for educated visitors.

Though it is difficult to accommodate, let alone please every type of individual, designers can at least consider the visitor profile and plan for traffic flow and modes of presentation accordingly. If the exhibition is one in which a family may wish to stick together, then content and interpretive techniques should be intermixed so that each age group will be engaged simultaneously within any given area. After all, if toddlers are bored and impatient, parents won't have the opportunity to absorb information at their own pace. Older children might fly by the text panels in search of greater stimulation, while their parents may rush through seeking a quiet place to sit where they are not assaulted by cacophony. Wouldn't it make sense to strive to create environments which not only address visitors' individual needs, but also offer them attractive opportunities to engage with the information together?

Finally, we must stress the absolute imperative that designers employ "universal design" in all their projects. Gone are the dark days when public venues could only be enjoyed by people with certain abilities. The concept of designing for "the handicapped" or "disabled" should also be relegated to the dust heap of history. People learn and interact in a myriad of ways suited to their physical and cognitive abilities. Universal design calls for us to provide

Remember the Children:
Daniel's Story, **United States**
Holocaust Memorial Museum
Designed by Darcy Fohrman. This
exhibition appeals to adults and
children alike by immersing the visitor
in a recreation of a specific experience,
using multiple layers of information.

equally enlightening and fulfilling experiences and opportunities for all. This includes recognizing that Braille, adequate lighting, type size, and color contrast constitute good graphic design. It means providing closed-captioning and infrared hearing assistance with audio. Explanatory signage should be "layered" in such a way that visitors with varied levels of reading ability, as well as different levels of interest and familiarity with the subject, are all stimulated and informed. There can be no place which is off limits to wheelchair users or those with walkers or canes. But much more than following these and other simple and absolutely necessary guidelines, we must as designers think broadly and deeply about who our visitors are and how we can create fully engaging environments which communicate with them on multiple levels, and as richly as possible.

Left: Feudi di San Gregorio booth, VinItalia Fair
Designed by Vignelli Associates. This trade show booth for a wine company uses several levels of detail, including a sculpture, a tasting experience, and an informational display. All facets engage the visitor and promote the product.

Below left: The National Underground Railroad Freedom Center
Designed by Jack Rouse Associates. This museum is designed to reach a very sophisticated audience by using the Underground Railroad as a means to explore a range of freedom issues. Interactive exhibits, films, and multimedia displays educate and reflect on the struggle for freedom through the eras of abolition, civil rights, and beyond.

Below right: The Liberty Bell Center
Designed by Ueland Junker McCauley Nicholson. This exhibition promotes access ability at a number of levels, including easy-to-access information, high-contrast lighting, and layering of content.

**Skin Tight: The
Sensibility of the Flesh,
Chicago Museum of
Contemporary Art**
Designed by Ammar Eloueini
Digit-all Studio. This exhibition
profiles fashion in a close and
intimate way by bringing the
exhibition down to the level
of the audience. The ability
to touch and feel helps
people to engage with
the exhibits.

The power of the new experience

In 1999 Six Sigma ruled the world. The business strategy formulated by Jack Welch of General Electric to cut costs and create more efficient operations was adopted in nearly every large retail operation at the expense of design.

It proved to be a failure. Modern consumers expect design excellence in product and presentation. Today, many companies have changed their strategy. Design and experience now stand at the center of business strategy.

With this trend afoot in the world of commerce, how has this affected exhibition design? The biggest change is that design is now a primary factor in the creation of exhibitions. Previously, museum exhibitions were defined by what they displayed and collected. Today, traveling shows and exhibitions are judged by the quality of their stories and presentation. There used to be no such job title as trade show booth designer and design was just an afterthought on the budget expense line. Now these designers are stars, and the design-build companies are catching up by investing ever greater amounts of their budget in the design stage. Investment in design quality through a longer process, better compensation, and better quality of materials and technology are filtering their way down from the elite to the everyday.

In 1974, Louis Kahn, the world famous architect, died in Pennsylvania Station, penniless and alone (or so the story goes).

Today, his contemporaries are creating mass market furniture for retailers and appear on the covers of international magazines. The star appeal that has jumped from clothes to products to architecture is now shaping exhibition design. Institutions are seeking out designers with international recognition to gain a competitive edge.

Exhibition design is also being impacted by the globalization of design. Through mass communication the design quality of exhibitions is improving throughout the world. High-quality museum exhibitions that may only have been seen in major design centers, such as London, Paris, and New York are now appearing in less-established markets, such as Malaysia, Korea, and South Africa. International traveling shows and trade show displays have also improved their design standards.

Up to this point we have led you to believe that design influence is a one way street, but this is not the case. Exhibitions themselves have also helped stir consumer demands for higher quality design in products and services. The popularization of showroom/retail spaces like Apple and Coach stores have promoted high-end products to a mass audience, and gallery exhibitions have advanced new movements in products as diverse as art, furniture, and automobiles. Demands for the new experience have shaped the exhibition and in return the exhibition has raised the bar for everything else.

Lanxess trade show booth, Berlin
Designed by bachman.kern & partner. Trade show exhibitions have evolved from simple product displays to vehicles for defining an organization's identity and view toward design. High-end trade shows are now common throughout the world.

Left: Target display
Designed by Random Productions. Target is known as a company that utilizes design in products to attain a competitive advantage in the discount store market. Often criticized for environments that do not match the quality of its products, this display is an attempt to use environmental design at a mass-market level.

Below: Clerc trade show booth, Basel
Designed by Pentagram. This design typifies the quality of materials used in high-end trade show exhibitions, especially for specialty product manufacturers such as Clerc. The movement toward using higher quality materials has been spurred by intense competition.

Left: The John Glenn Institute
Designed by Eyethink. Exhibition design quality has escalated even for day-to-day working environments. This exhibition is architecturally integrated into an academic building.

Below: *Big & Green: Toward Sustainable Architecture in the 21st Century*, National Building Museum
Designed by James Hicks, graphics designed by Pure+Applied. Exhibitions such as this one have helped to popularize sustainability for a mass audience.

Everything old is new again

When we look at the myriad advances in the use of digital media in museum, retail, and trade show environments, we often forget that the underlying principles behind these technologies have been around for hundreds of years. With a short survey of the history of communication devices in exhibitions, it becomes increasingly evident that while the technology may have changed, the application has stayed fundamentally the same.

The magic lantern and the cyclorama

During the nineteenth century, the magic lantern wowed audiences with projected images, telling a story in an immersive space, while the cyclorama introduced the same concept using large-scale paintings to create an immersive experience. The Kodak Pavilion in the 1939–1940 New York World's Fair duplicated the same experience using lit images in a theater in-the-round. LED and projection screens are the modern day equivalents of these slide shows, and are now common devices in museums, visitor centers, and themed amusements. Incredibly though, while the technology has changed, the application of that technology has remained remarkably consistent, with an inverse theater in-the-round still a commonly-used feature. A public space where the reactions of fellow audience members can be seen and shared, is still seen as an attraction to visitors.

The moving and interactive image

Since the 1930s, incorporating moving images into an exhibition has been the goal of most progressive designers. Starting with costly and unreliable 16mm film, jumping to difficult-to-maintain U-matic videotape and then progressing to Laserdiscs, DVDs, Video Servers, and now Solid State Players, through each advance in technology designers have recreated the exhibition experience to exploit the advantages of new media. Designers have generally used moving image technology to push the exhibition in two directions; the large-scale spectacle, and the immersive environment. In both cases successful application rests with giving the visitor a holistic storytelling experience, with the image as a key support.

The Crown Fountain, Millennium Park
Designed by Jaume Plensa. This fountain in Chicago's Millenium Park is a modern example of the moving image as spectacle. It consists of two 50 foot (15.2m) glass block towers, which include LED screens that project video images of local citizens.

China Millenium Monument

Designed by Electrosonic and Measure Scientific. As spectacles grow larger and larger, audiences are demanding more realistic displays. The China Millenium Monument in Beijing incorporates this projection videowall, which uses the VECTOR™ image-processing system. VECTOR™ was used because it can display images of any type and size without any degradation of quality.

Immersion

The guided tour is one of the oldest interpretive devices in exhibitions, bringing an unprecedented level of interaction. The use of human guides to tell compelling stories will never be truly replaced, but the use of kiosks, personal digital assistants, and the internet has enriched the storytelling experience. A new development is that audience reactions and additional stories can be archived and used to expand the experience, while adding additional imagery and depth. In this environment, the live tour guide can become a channel, taking the rich archive of experience and adding their own personal spin.

What conclusions can we draw from these histories? The most important is that, with all the changes in technology over the centuries, the way people perceive and enjoy space has remained remarkably similar. The desire to be surrounded by a story in a public space, to be told stories dynamically, and to have an interactive experience blended with real environments will forever drive design decisions. This means that no matter how far technology progresses, tried and true methods will still be used. The power of the human voice, the electricity of being surrounded by an audience, and the excitement of using light for movement will always have their places among the digital devices and holographic images.

The Washington-Rochambeau Revolutionary Route
Designed by Talisman Interactive. This heritage trail extends from New York to Virginia to commemorate and interpret the route taken by George Washington's troops to attack the British army at Yorktown. The interactive kiosks, maps, and cellphone information systems interpret an historic environment that is invisible to the eye in most cases, using technology to interpret place, instead of graphics and stage sets. The project looks to a future where technology can help interpret and archive multiple levels of meaning in one place. Hundreds or thousands of possible interpretations can occur in this environment.

The Museum of Tolerance
Designed by Houghton Kneale Design. Interactive elements have become further and further integrated with the complete exhibition design. The advent of personal digital assistants has made technological integration almost seamless.

What makes a public space an exhibition?

What makes a public space that communicates? This question often stirs a debate among architects, designers, and historians. Don't all spaces interpret some time or place? This may be true, but the difference of great spaces that communicate is the focus on one central story. That story can already exist with very little intervention, such as ancient ruins or house museums, or can be a new creation.

A great interpretive public space allows the audience to tune out the message and use the space simply as a place of enjoyment and relaxation. Places like the Eastbank Esplanade in Portland, Oregon, have high-quality interpretive elements and connect the user with the environment, but the vast majority of visitors use the place just to sit and enjoy the day.

A great space that communicates also needs to fulfill the narrative objectives of the institution creating or managing the space. This often creates confusion between the needs of celebrating great architecture and the specific needs of the institution. The Tate Modern in London or the Musée d'Orsay in Paris are great public environments and vessels for exhibitions that interpret art; but do these buildings communicate a specific institutional story in their own right, or do they have to reconcile many narratives including the history of the building, its place in the environment, and its multiple functions?

The Forum, Rome
The Forum is an exciting display of public art and space unparalleled in the world. Elements that survived the centuries are carefully arranged to interpret what once existed with almost no additional interpretive devices. With that decision, the Forum not only represents what once was, but also how what is left serves as a center in modern Rome. The Forum is meant to be a place that impresses with its raw power, while leaving open a number of questions that can be answered through additional research.

Left: Eastbank Esplanade Urban Markers
Designed by Mayer Reed. The Urban Marker project is part of the Eastbank Esplanade, a riverfront pedestrian and bicycle corridor. Twenty foot (6m) tall stainless steel structures mark the 13 intersections where city streets historically met the riverfront; the Urban Markers incorporate street signs, luminaires, and story panels. Each of the Urban Marker story panels is seen in juxtaposition with architectural remnants of the area's industrial past. Where possible, historic images are closely matched to the current views. The Esplanade's mix of a highly used urban space with interpretive elements integrates the project with its community. The history of the place can be engaged with at any time by the public.

Right: Pennsylvania Military Museum
Designed by Purdy O'Gwynn Architects. This 100 foot (30.5m) long front facade depicts military service ribbons in full color. The facade thus becomes an outdoor educational exhibit and a point of orientation and connection between the various site features, creating the central node for the park, memorials, and museum.

But is it art?

We see art all around us, from sculptures by famous artists to memorials and local landmarks that define a community and create a sense of place. Public art that communicates goes one step beyond defining a place through art to interpreting a point in time, a community, or an issue. The art piece must accomplish this goal without becoming a museum or exhibition that creates its own context.

Artists delicately straddle the line between art and exhibition by using the tools at their disposal: landscape, architecture, space, and community. By drawing on the environment, artists allow art to become a mirror on the outside world. The work is meant to be approached and engaged with, without ignoring the surrounding environment and the emotions the visitor brings with them.

Monuments to wars, great events, and tragedies are the most common public art pieces balancing the act of storytelling with serving the needs of a community landmark. The Vietnam Veterans Memorial by Maya Lin is often held up as the model for how a monument to war dead can communicate a message about war using abstract elements, but in the end its success had much to do with its reinvention of the landmark from a place to be admired from a distance, to an engaging experience that forces the visitor to become a close observer and explorer.

Vietnam Veterans Memorial
Designed by Maya Lin.

Left: *Work-Shift/Chicago*
Designed by Krivanek+Breaux
Art+Design. Twenty-eight
massive wooden posts stand
in an orderly rectangular
configuration. The east and
west faces of the posts are
inscribed with the job titles of
members of the community.
The north and south sides are
inscribed with words these
workers use to explain their
job experience. The north has
negative descriptions and the
south has positive words. The
skeletal configuration of the
blackened posts mirrors the
massive, unoccupied factory
structure across the street.
Collectively, the posts can be
seen to represent an animal
pen or penitentiary, a
vanishing yet habitable space,
a community or a grave,
marking the almost complete
death of industrial Chicago.

Above: Isurava Memorial
Designed by Hewitt Pender
Associates. Memorials are
areas where space and
landscape interpret the past
and commemorate fallen
heroes. For this memorial
commemorating the 60th
anniversary of a battle in New
Guinea, four black, Australian
granite sentinel stones, each
weighing 3½ tons, were
airlifted by helicopter for
installation. Each stone is
inscribed with a single word
representing the values and
qualities of those soldiers who
fought on the Kokoda Track.
A platform looking out over
the valley is concealed from
the top memorial tier. This
lower platform contains 10
interpretive panels describing
the time frame and significance
of the event, and also pays
tribute to the local people.

Light installation, Neue Nationalgalerie

Designed by Jenny Holzer and Sunrise Systems. Like much of her work, Holzer's installation at Berlin's Neue Nationalgalerie was made for a specific space and designed to last a particular length of time. However, this exhibition has since become a permanent part of the gallery. The use of LED displays as art parallels the elegant, abstract structure of the gallery building designed by Mies van der Rohe. The 13 LED displays were installed on the ceiling grid of the great hall; each is over 160 feet (48.7m) long for a total of 2,200 feet (670.6m). They hang 26 feet (7.9m) in the air and use a total of 701,792 amber LEDs. The signs were programmed in mirrored text with alternating speed. Using a ratio of sign speed and letter height, the appearance of the gallery roof was made even more dramatic; visual effects simulated the roof to bow, appear concave, convex, and even twisted.

CoReFab, traveling exhibition (top two images) and *Nubi-Verdopolis*, Steel Case Building (bottom two images) Designed by Ammar Eloueini Digit-all Studio. The exhibition design work of Ammar Eloueini straddles the line between interpretation and art through a strong use of sculpture and materials. Display elements float in space in high tension, demanding to be read along with the information in the display.

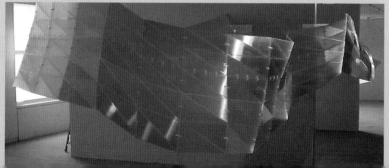

Experience design and themed environments

A concept and design process called "experience design" has long been a buzzword in the exhibition and environment design fields. Experience design has been used to explain everything from a process of developing products and services around customer behaviors, to developing unique educational models. Is experience design really unique though, or is it a design process that has evolved as a more advanced version of traditional storytelling that has existed for hundreds of years?

Are themed environments experience design?

Experience design in environments has often been described as incorporating passive storytelling, nonlinear educational experiences, and interactive engagement with visitors. These concepts though have been around for the past 150 years and are in fact the central tenants of themed environments. World's Fairs starting in the mid-1800s, and amusement parks in the twentieth century used performance, detail, immersive environments, and public space to create memorable educational experiences. The skill and craft involved in creating these environments have become institutionalized in certain design regions, such as southern California with its large number of movie studios and theme parks, and Stockholm and Copenhagen with their concentration of toy and furniture manufacturers.

Why is experience design different?

Experience design is different from developing themed environments in a number of fundamental ways. This does not mean that experience design does not incorporate many of the values of theming. Experience design takes the concept of themed storytelling deeper, while questioning the nature of how environments communicate in a number of ways, which we will now examine.

Utilizing nontraditional models

Themed environments have fundamentally been a craft developed by designers using familiar models for environmental storytelling that have evolved over time. IDEO's Fred Dust defines a key tenant of experience design as looking outside of traditional project types, turning a trade show display into a museum space, or looking at a retail display like a classroom.

Designing for behaviors

Demographics are considered a primary tool for the development of design concepts for audiences. Increasingly however, life states are not in line with age states and shared attitudes across generations suggest new ways to design. By looking at behaviors as a key to designing experiences, environments cut through demographic barriers.

**US Pavilion, 2005
World Expo, Japan**
Designed by BRC
Imagination Arts. World's
Fairs were the first themed
environments, enclosing and
encapsulating an experience
under one roof. In this pavilion,
visitors were immersed in
a storyline and experience
focusing on the life and
work of Benjamin Franklin.

Including audience input

Themed exhibitions are often passive, but adding interactive elements can dynamically change an exhibition. Advances in technology have enhanced this trend in recent years, with the internet capable of creating customized personal unique experience with users (most clearly seen with websites like MySpace). Participatory experiences are commonly used in children's museums, where children can add to or construct environments that fundamentally alter the exhibit. Interactive elements are also used in exhibitions dedicated to current events, which often have spaces for visitors to add their comments, which are then incorporated into the display.

Designing for time, not place

Experience design focuses on the experience of the audience over time, not just in the exhibition space. This often materializes as exhibitions that include ongoing publications, discussion groups, shows, and summaries.

Reinforce learning with dialogue

The experience design process does not assume that audiences have understood the educational content or story behind an exhibition. By supporting dialogue through audience input or interpreter facilitation, the exhibition experience is incorporated into an ongoing conversation.

ONS (The Offshore Northern Seas Foundation) exhibition
Designed by Ammar Eloueini Digit-all Studio and Fasett.

This design reflects the Norwegian landscape, with offshore petroleum and gas installations, the sea, and mountain ranges. The project brings advances in experience design to the forefront by using abstract sculptural imagery to reflect landscape and climate.

IMAGE ECONOMIES

The human nervous system evolved in an environment where seeing change – the slightest difference in the surrounding environment – could mean the difference between life and death. So it is not surprising that our most developed cultural forms are practices of the visual. But we didn't stop there. So much of life occurs outside the range of visible light. Through scientific tools and methods we have reached far beyond this narrow slice of the electromagnetic spectrum to colonize its full range, from radio waves and infrared to x-rays, gamma radiation and cosmic rays. Now, existence in all its glorious complexity, from the dynamic division of living cells to the vastness and vibrancy of the entire known universe, has been rendered accessible to our visual capacity. Meanwhile, the democratization of the means for making and sharing images in the cultural realm continues to explode exponentially. As cost approaches zero and access to image production and dissemination becomes universal, new possibilities begin to emerge. Our insatiable embrace of the image knows no bounds.

Massive Change, The Vancouver Art Gallery
Designed by Bruce Mau Design and the Institute Without Boundaries. The work and writings of Bruce Mau Design exemplifies the farthest philosophical reaches of experience design. His exhibitions force the audience to take a stand on a subject, and be fully engaged before, during, and after the exhibition. The *Massive Change* exhibition is accompanied by a website and book, making the exhibition just one tool in an overall experience.

Designing from the ground up and the inside out

The potential for environmental storytelling is unlimited by scale. One can co-opt a city, a campus, a building, an exhibition, a trade show booth, or a sign and put any of them in service to specific interpretive goals. Of course, in reality our venue and scope are often dictated to us, and we strive to squeeze out of them all the narrative and symbolic juice that they offer.

A particular dichotomy presented to exhibition designers is the variable of intervening with an already designed or built space versus having input into the creation of that space before the exhibition is developed. For those who have had the good fortune to be involved in the latter situation, the empowerment and potential for meaning-making are intoxicating and addictive. Every aspect of the design of a site and building can be brought to bear on the act of communication. Elements such as location; procession; entry; circulation; form, height, width, and depth of space; qualities of light, both natural and artificial; materials; details; structure; climate control; and even security are all fertile ground for the quality and degree of interpretation achieved.

Even in new projects though, the building's design often comes first. Fundraisers find it easier to attract donations to the bright, shiny creation of a "star architect" rather than the messier and more complex description of an exhibition program. The designer should seek to establish a relationship between the exhibition experience and its envelope. If the building is designed, but not yet constructed, fight to influence the design, as necessitated by the expressive and technical requirements of the exhibition. In an existing space, do a thorough analysis of every aspect that can be brought into play in the creation of a clear and holistic narrative.

When working to integrate an exhibition with its environment, remember that buildings, parks, and landscapes serve multiple functions beyond telling a story: many museums' main function is actually holding weddings! Buildings and landscapes are also wrapped up in the identity of a city and an architect. The Guggenheim museum in New York has been chastised for its lack of exhibition flexibility, but its architecture is also a major part of its appeal. The museum is a legacy of an architect's philosophy and sometimes an exhibition needs to bow to that reality.

So whether starting from scratch or working inside an existing building, design from the inside out. Over time, people have dumbed down the architect Louis Sullivan's adage that "form follows function," missing his deeper intention concerning the potential for every aspect of a building's design to embody a broad range of meanings related to its inherent purpose. When we design truly interpretive exhibits, we must understand that proceeding from the inside out means discovering and exploiting every creative opportunity to let the whole environment speak.

The Museum of the American Indian

Designed by Douglas Cardinal Architects, GBQC Architects, and Johnpaul Jones. The role of some museum buildings is to house multiple exhibitions by many different design firms. This does not mean though that the building should be designed outside the realm of the story. In the case of this large museum, the early stakeholder process defined a number of themes that would be reflected in both the exhibitions, the building, and the grounds.

Merck headquarters
Designed by Ueland Junker McCauley Nicholson. "Branded environments" is a term that describes the merger of architecture, space, and corporate identity. A corporate exhibition is yet another layer to add to these environments. Telling a story inside a lobby or office space requires careful integration of informational elements into the floors, walls, lighting systems, and building circulation.

Cincinnati Museum of Art
Designed by Zaha Hadid.
Art museums are one area
where the architecture
can have a big impact on
exhibition development. In
the case of this building, the
internal circulation is extruded
to the outside, giving the
visitor an understanding of
the nature of the exhibition
space within. The building
demands a creative response
from the exhibition designer.
Exhibitions need to adapt to
the power of this environment
to be successful.

Anatomy

Exhibitions are developed to represent the culture, document the trends, or establish the historical narrative of a certain place and time. Throughout history exhibitions have taken on many forms to support various institutions, ranging from churches to monarchies and cities. This section of the book will explore the nature of contemporary exhibitions and the institutions they support, including museums, corporations, educational facilities, and government entities.

While all exhibitions use the environment to communicate, they diverge in the goals of their narratives. Educational museum exhibitions focus on interpreting a specific subject, theme, or story; while corporate and institutional exhibitions use interpretation as a marketing device or to support a place. Trade shows and showroom displays are the most focused, marketing a specific product or service. These different goals not only reflect in diverging narrative approaches, but also in how much money will be invested, the duration of the design process, the nature of the collaborative effort, and the longevity of the final product.

If there is a common thread among the divergent disciplines it is in the design process itself. Exhibitions may tell different stories in different environments, but they are consistent in the way they require collaborative effort to succeed, their need for a clear narrative approach, and the way they have to balance the needs of creating a space with communicating a message.

Savane africaine

Exhibition design for museums

Museum design is a specialized form of exhibition planning that is content-driven, informative, educational, and entertaining. Museum design is also a very varied discipline: exhibitions can be permanent or temporary, the design time frame can range from a few months to two or three years. The designer may coordinate the architecture, interior design, and exhibition design for the whole museum, creating an integrated and seamless design. More commonly, however, the designer will just be involved in designing an exhibition within an existing facility.

The content of museum exhibitions can be timeless and can be in place for decades, so the narrative and the design need to remain valid. This narrative must be accessible to all the various audience types who will visit the museum: children, teens, adults, and the elderly. The design may utilize a combination of static/passive and dynamic/interactive components to provide varying levels of entry points into the story. The exhibition can live in the physical environment, but can also extend into the virtual world via the internet as an educational resource to be used before or after the site visit.

Designing for museums is an activity that necessarily engages with the architecture and interior design of the building which houses the exhibition. In particular, the collaboration between all team members is critical in developing new museums since exhibitions can drive the architecture and interior design into a holistic design scheme. Of course, topic-oriented exhibitions are most commonly designed into existing museums.

Whether working with a space in an existing building or crafting a completely new space from the inside out, the designer scripts the story within the planned or existing traffic patterns. Many exhibitions rely on telling a sequence of events linearly. Explicitly linear storytelling can be different from the traditional art museum exhibition, which might allow visitors to browse or go directly to the piece that specifically interests them. The linear narrative exhibit is directed, as in Washington DC's National Holocaust Museum (see page 194) where visitors venture down a given path as a group at a controlled rate. In this case, the museum was developed from the inside out and the story it tells is permanent and unchanging. Of course, the designer can craft a special exhibition into an existing museum to be similarly experienced, but the designer must keep in mind how it affects existing and adjacent exhibitions. Curators, registrars, education specialists, and funders are often part of the exhibition review process during the various phases of design.

Mixing Messages: Graphic Design in Contemporary Culture, **Cooper-Hewitt National Design Museum** Designed and curated by Ellen Lupton.

History museums

History museums document notable events from the past and answer the question "what happened?" They give us a richer knowledge of culture and offer clues about how society has developed. Numerous exhibitions may occur simultaneously within one museum space and can cover a range of time periods. Within individual exhibitions, narratives are usually based on chronology and topic, which lends well to designing linear paths for visitors.

Historical exhibitions may rely on text, artifacts, and archival images to tell stories. Designers and content developers (sometimes they are the same) must select the right amount of these elements to tell the story successfully and engage visitors from differing age ranges and backgrounds.

Living on the River Han, **Gyeonggi Provincial Museum**
Designed by Design IGA. Nearly every town or city around the world has a museum dedicated to local history, giving the community a way to both archive its history and welcome visitors. This exhibition presents traditional life on the River Han in Korea. Using simple modular glass cases, the display of objects is given a sense of power and grace.

International Spy Museum
Designed by Gallagher
Associates. The International
Spy Museum may represent
the future of museum
exhibitions. Part theme park
ride, part education center,
and part history museum, the
central focus on espionage
can be taken in numerous
directions. A for-profit
museum that must keep a
steady stream of visitors in
order to survive, it must
always try to remain relevant
to new generations of visitors.

Right and above: *Pearls*, American Museum of Natural History

Designed by the American Museum of Natural History's exhibition department. Both a science and a history museum, the American Museum of Natural History has a large in-house exhibition design department skilled in object display as well as media and interior design. Many of their exhibitions integrate object displays with interactive computer kiosks to make a visual connection that is successfully followed up at deeper levels. These exhibitions are excellent examples of the use of multiple levels of display information to captivate visitors. The museum also works with leading design firms like Pentagram and Ralph Appelbaum Associates on their large-scale projects.

Right: Imperial War Museum North

Building by Daniel Libeskind. Architecture by Alistair McCall Real Studios. This museum tells the story of how war has affected the lives of British and Commonwealth citizens since 1914. Constantly moving light is projected against the building and the artifacts inside to create a powerful effect.

Pro Football Hall of Fame
Designed by DMCD. Halls of
fame have been increasingly
popular in North America
since the National Baseball
Hall of Fame opened in
Cooperstown, New York
in 1939. There are now halls
of fame that profile sports,
teams, themes, and cities.
While they are all different
in their subjects, they all
contain one consistent
display element: the story
of a single person (the
inductee), using a mix of
sculpture, object, and text
to explain their importance.

Science museums

Science museums help to answer the question, "how?" Science is a living subject and new research and studies are continuously emerging. Science exhibitions are content-driven with topics, at times, up for debate. They provoke thought and raise public awareness. Exhibition design firms must create memorable experiences for visitors and translate scientific content into a form that the general public can easily digest. Trends in design for science museums have moved from passive and static contemplative displays to dynamic, hands-on experiences. Through interactivity, motion, experimentation, and sensory experiences, visitors learn by doing.

The key is to turn complex information into an accessible and immersive experience. Scientific data is often seen as complicated and dry. Designers can introduce artistic, creative, and appropriately whimsical exhibits in order to break this stereotype.

Grande Galerie de L'evolution, French National Natural History Museum
Designed by Chemetov & Huidobro. Nothing captivates an audience like large-scale elements arranged in an even larger space. This exhibition releases life-size models of animals and allows them to roam the floor, using the displays to divide the space and impart a greater understanding of the differences between animals.

**The Body Fantastic,
Odyssium**

Designed by AldrichPears
Associates. This exhibition
invites visitors to stroll
through a carnival and test
their strengths, skills, and
senses while learning about
the wonders of the human
body. Colorful sideshow
banners "pitch" basic
anatomy and body systems.
Games of skill and chance
provide opportunities to mimic
body processes. The carnival
theme provided a graphic
approach that appealed to all
the target audience groups,
but especially the primary
audience: teenagers who
usually avoid such exhibitions.

City of Science and Industry, Parc de la Villette
Designed by Adrien Fainsilber and Bernard Tschumi. Related to Tschumi's theoretical work on "event space," this design for a distinctly urban park and science museum in Paris called for the deployment of a number of abstract, programless structures, dubbed "follies." The science museum is designed to flow in and out of the park space.

Adventure Aquarium
Designed by Communication Arts. Zoos and aquariums have changed from being immersive animal habitats to highly interpretive educational centers. Exhibitions in these environments now utilize techniques traditionally found in art galleries and history museums.

Art museums

Art museums are both educational and entertaining attractions, but also provide the most passive visitor experience. They display two-dimensional works, sculptures, multimedia works, or installations for visitors to contemplate and interpret. A museum's in-house staff of curators and educational departments generally decide the layout of artwork in galleries. Exhibition design for art museums can range from simple painted walls with text panels to decadent interior designs that emphasize the characteristics of the art, such as the period in which it was created. Museum staff may outsource exhibition design for specialized cases, such as traveling exhibitions, children's sections, or interior architecture.

Art and architecture have had a symbiotic relationship since the beginning of civilization, and art museums take advantage of adventurous architecture. The museum building can be as much of an attraction as the artwork inside. Exhibitions can be organized randomly, chronologically, by genre, or by artist. Visitors tend to wander through art museums in a random path when a museum offers compartmentalized galleries, leading to the design of new museum spaces that offer a more subtle transition of spaces with changing lighting, graphics, and displays.

Museo di Castelvecchio
Designed by Carlo Scarpa. Scarpa was ahead of his time as one of the first architects to gain fame mainly through exhibition design commissions, including showrooms, tombs, and museums. A master of object display, Scarpa configured the sculptures in this museum on pedestals of varying sizes to frame them in different views.

Art museum architecture

The architecture of an art museum can often dominate the organization of its exhibitions, by mandating a specific circulation and organization of display spaces. The challenge for the exhibition designer is not only to work within the special confines, but also to turn them to their advantage.
Below: Guggenheim New York, designed by Frank Lloyd Wright
Right: Guggenheim Bilbao, designed by Frank Gehry and Associates

Audrey Jones Beck Building, The Museum of Fine Arts Houston
Designed by Vignelli Associates. A master of typography, Massimo Vignelli used the subtle naming of galleries, displays, and donor recognitions to reinforce the power of the modern architectural space.

Russel Wright: Creating American Lifestyle, Cooper-Hewitt National Design Museum
Designed by Matter Practice. Ellen Lupton, the Curator of the Cooper-Hewitt National Design Museum is a leading patron and designer of object-driven art displays. Housed in a former mansion, the numerous exhibitions held at the museum combine interior design, furniture design, and environmental graphics in a potent and intriguing mix at a small scale.

Children's museums

When designing for a children's exhibition, all design aspects have to be centered around interaction. Designing based on age group interests is critical; what interests a toddler is worlds away from what interests the average 10-year old. Most designers have age ranges and topics in mind for specific pieces. Research and observation of kids at play can help establish the goals for an exhibition. Exhibitions can engage their audience by including play: a physical, social, or isolated activity that helps children learn through creativity and experimentation.

With children being the target audience, the designer must also pay close attention to scale, durability, and safety. Watchful parents prefer to be able to see their child from any vantage point in a space, so permeable or minimal barriers are desirable. The layout of a children's museum can be fairly random, with differing age-leveled exhibits scattered throughout a space. There is no strong need for a linear path as there is for a historical exhibition.

**Paradise Valley
Children's Playcourt**
Designed by Thinking Caps.
This court features a
collection of huge soft play
objects, all representing five
healthy lifestyle choices for
kids: fresh air, exercise, good
food, education, and rest.

V&A Museum of Childhood
Designed by Caruso St. John.
The designers worked with
the V&A on a long-term
transformation of this
Victorian museum. The
renovated space is more
welcoming and has better
access. Historical and
modern toys are displayed
with reverence and grace.

Public centers are distinct from museums in the nature of their purpose, audience, and content. Public centers include visitor centers, corporate museums, institutional centers, parks, and heritage centers. In these exhibitions, the designer crafts a narrative that focuses on the mission and goals, the products, and the philosophy of the organization. The design needs to accommodate periodic updates and enhancements and be easily modifiable as mission statements shift.

Visitor centers attract varied audiences and can become synonymous with the cities in which they are located. A corporate museum or institutional center can be more cerebral and targeted toward adults; they both focus on a particular brand or institution, but can also attract a wide variety of audiences.

The exhibition life span in these types of venues can be from five to seven years and is often updated annually in some way. Interactive media can add easily updatable elements that do not require building or rebuilding of the physical space. Some exhibition types have designated areas that are frequently changed in order to draw return visitors. The designer's involvement in these exhibitions can be as extensive as coordinating with building architects and interior designers. In renovation cases, the space is allotted, but the modification of the space is key so that the traffic pattern is established based on how the story needs to be told.

Capitoline Hill
This large-scale Renaissance project, developed by Michelangelo, was not only one of the world's first museums, but also became an early unofficial visitor center, mediating between the contemporary city and the ancient Roman forum that had been recently uncovered. The display of antiquities in the courtyard and the formal staircase beyond work to introduce visitors to the glory of ancient Rome.

Visitor centers

Visitor centers are the most broad category of public centers, and can overlap with corporate or institutional museums. The aim of visitor centers is to highlight attractions for their audience, but they can also serve as attractions in their own right. They generally do not cater to any specialized audience like a corporate or institutional museum may do. Visitor centers attract a very wide range of people and the space has to be designed accordingly.

The information in a visitor center can be presented sequentially like a book, where the story evolves. To achieve this, the path of the visitor must be managed, destinations need to be focused, and sound needs to be controlled. In contrast, a visitor center can also be a browsing environment where parts of the story are open to passing traffic.

Sears Tower Skydeck
Designed by Hunt Design with Dellmont Leisure and Michael Devine. Often visitor centers focus on what is being developed in the future as much as what already exists. This display inside Sears Tower shows the past, present, and future of Chicago.

North Mountain Interpretive Center
Designed by Thinking Caps. This center provides a great deal of interpretive information inside of a small space by integrating an exhibition system kit of parts into wayfinding and identity signs, as well as interior details.

Tillamook Forest Center
Designed by AldrichPears Associates with Miller Hull and Walker Macy. From 1933 to 1951 a series of devastating fires burned vast areas of Tillamook Forest. This land has since been restored to become one of the best examples of a sustainably managed forest. The Center contains theatrical and interactive experiences centered on forest management. As with most successful visitor centers, the interior displays are closely linked to the external environment, with outdoor views playing a role in the interactive experience.

Old Faithful Visitor Education Center, Yellowstone National Park

Designed by Christopher Chadbourne & Associates. The designers worked with the National Park Service and a team of scientists and educators to develop the exhibits for the Old Faithful Visitor Education Center. The aim of the Center is to introduce visitors to the complex science underlying the hydrothermal and microbiological activity in Yellowstone.

Independence Visitor Center

Designed by Gallagher & Associates. One of the largest visitor centers in the world, this exhibition must serve three duties: orienting visitors to Independence National Historical Park, the city of Philadelphia, and the surrounding region. The designers created a colorful signage system that accents the subdued interiors of the building. Graphics are used to highlight Philadelphia's colonial history.

Corporate museums

Corporate museums are typically located in a company's headquarters or at a major manufacturing plant, and their aim is to display a corporation's history and philosophy. A corporate museum can serve as a visual for what a company stands for and can also be a tool for promoting the corporation to clients and the public.

These museums can target a niche audience, such as company staff and clients, or can be open to the general public. The most common mistake a corporation can make is not training their staff in corporate culture. Without this knowledge, staff cannot effectively promote the brand; corporate museums help to educate staff.

The design of corporate displays can often follow the techniques commonly used in art museums, so that products are displayed like precious artifacts, and vintage ads like paintings. Most corporations are continually evolving, so the museums need to be designed to be flexible and adaptable. They need to accommodate new corporate divisions, consolidations, and mergers. A company's mission and goals also evolve. Designers can plan for these changes dynamically through the use of multimedia and computer technology. The exhibition design of a corporate museum can usually start as soon as architectural planning begins, so it can be integrated seamlessly.

Robert Mondavi Winery
Designed by West Office Exhibition Design. For exhibitions featuring tours of attractive industrial plants like wineries, less is often more. This tour reveals the history and inner workings of the Robert Mondavi Winery. Beginning in the vineyard, visitors follow grapes throughout their vine-to-wine life cycle. They peer from atop fermentation tanks, wind down through the barrel room, and explore the cellar. The graphics are elegant, but minimal, enhancing the experience of being part of a working facility.

P&G headquarters

Designed by Kolar Design. This project was developed to introduce visitors to the extensive number of brands that make up P&G, and to represent the company's history and core values. A characterless space has been transformed into a spirited, branded experience. The integration of architecture, interiors, and branding is seamless through the use of color, shape, and materials. The exhibition immerses the visitor upon arrival by using every available surface of the space. The addition of comfortable furniture and cafes that closely align with the exhibition further reinforces the experience of the lobby space, providing an impressive entry for business and casual visitors.

Left: SPAM Museum
Designed by Design Craftsmen. This museum was designed in a tongue-in-cheek fashion, taking the visitor through the history of this product, its success in feeding the US troops during WWII, and its path to becoming a globally recognized product. The linear sequence of the museum directs the visitor to sit in the theater, walk the prescribed path, and taste the product hot off the frying pan, while the spam song by Monty Python accompanies the visitor on the way to the gift shop.

Below: BMW Zentrum
Designed by Context Design Group. In some cases, a corporation may choose to build a separate, freestanding pavilion as BMW did for its museum. Located next to a manufacturing plant, Zentrum displays the past, present, and future of BMW.

Petrosains Discovery Centre, Petronas Twin Towers
Designed by DMCD. Located in the base of the Petronas Twin Towers in Kuala Lumpur, the Petrosains Discovery Centre focuses on the Malaysian petroleum industry. Numerous interactive experiences transport visitors through geological time where they learn about petroleum formation, exploration, drilling procedures, and the mining market. The goal of the museum is to increase awareness of the petroleum industry and potential careers.

Institutional centers

These exhibitions serve as the "front door" to an institution, presenting museum-quality displays that articulate culture and values, and link an organization's past and present with its vision for the future. They reinforce brand loyalty, but with educational and public service components that go beyond marketing a product.

Institutional centers serve as places of orientation for employees and visitors, and as settings for high-level events. They answer the questions: "Who are we?"

"What do we stand for?" and "What makes us different?" They communicate an ethic, serving as a means to mentor new colleagues, reinforce commitment among employees and customers, and transmit values across the generations. Such exhibitions feel as if they come from the heart of an organization. A prestigious location along with high-quality displays and a color palette that reflects corporate standards all give a sense of respect and stature to an exhibition.

The Walter and Leonore Annenberg Science Center Designed by Hillier Group. This educational facility opened with an exhibition built in. The design approach was to engage the students on many levels. No matter where students and visitors go in the building, they are surrounded by science, with sculpture, interpretive panels, and diagrams integrated into floors, walls, and spaces.

These displays express key messages, but in a warm and understated way. The most effective exhibitions tell the great stories of an organization: the lives and achievements of their founders, how the organization overcame adversity, its contributions to the public good, and where the organization is headed in the future.

A sense of humility and a sense of humor are important to the design of these exhibitions. Some of the most powerful artifacts to display are modest, such as personal items from the founders or the early sketch of a major product. Perhaps most importantly, these exhibitions are no place for hagiography. Visitors enjoy learning about foibles and faux pas in addition to sterling accomplishments. An institution that can laugh—or at least smile—at itself is a healthy place to work and visit.

Donor wall, Baylor College of Medicine

Designed by Christina Wallach. Donor walls often tell the story of an institution. In this case, glass and light was the medium used to define the institution as a caring "family" within a world community. The Baylor Missions, with their tone of hope and broad scope, are placed within the context of Baylor's history timeline, the Baylor community of philanthropists, and the miraculous changing face of medicine. The effect is a richly textured and fluid "tapestry" of design.

 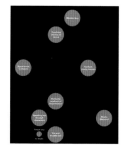 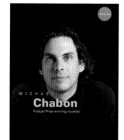 

Above: Legacy Gallery, University of Pittsburgh

Designed by Thoughtform. Utilizing a process of storyboarding with the client, followed by a detailed analysis of prospective users, Thoughtform developed a cylindrical electronic kiosk that matched the architectural detailing of the building interior. The kiosk consisted of a series of touchscreens containing profiles of famous University of Pittsburgh alumni in the worlds of art, medicine, science, and politics. The kiosk also contains an electronic directory of alumni.

Right: Donor wall, Kent State University Academic All-American Athletic Center

Designed by Amir Khosravi and Jerad Lavey. This low-budget project creates an environment that reflects both outstanding athletic and academic achievements. The exhibition is integrated into the existing interior space and uses subtle graphics.

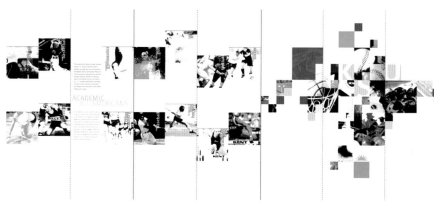

Parks, heritage centers, and botanical gardens

Outdoor environments are among the most difficult to interpret, because the goal is often to create as natural, seamless, and uncontrolled a place as possible. Added to these difficulties is the harshness of outdoor variables, such as weather, animals, sunlight, and pollution. For heritage centers, the difficulty is in interpreting places that may no longer exist or have been substantially altered by modern developments.

Successful exhibitions often tread lightly over the land, employing a multileveled design vocabulary that may take the form of individual objects or be integrated into walls or sidewalks. Signage also plays a significant role in these environments, discreetly assisting with navigating and providing a visual map of a place. This need to create a visual picture contrasts with museums and centers where navigation is often along a prescribed path, and the audience are completely focused on a story.

With recent upgrades in communication and information technology, such as cellphones and personal digital assistants, there has been a movement to connect large-scale heritage areas to specific themes with personal and relatable narratives. The physical exhibits in these cases are only a tiny part of the environment and can be integrated into visitor centers, house museums, or even educational and retail facilities.

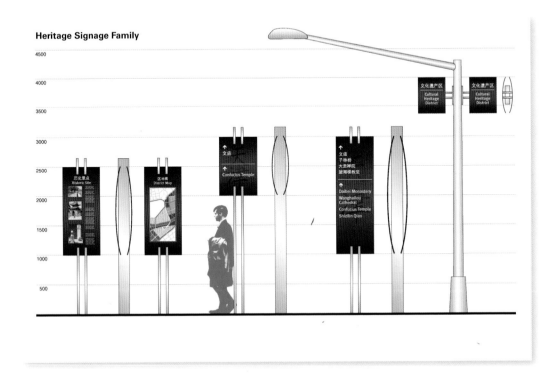

Heritage Signage Family

Opposite page: Tainjin Haihe River sign system
Designed by Calori & Vanden-Eynden. This sign system for the rapidly growing city of Tainjin in China, interprets a city in the process of being developed. By interpreting historic sites along with new buildings, the system can grow and change as needed.

Right and below: *Artificial Shrubbery, Luleå International Sculpture Biennale*, **Nordbatten Museum garden**
Designed by Irina Nakhova. This outdoor art installation shows the subtle balance between public art, public space, and interpretive installation.

Below and right: Oregon Children's Garden
Designed by Mayer/Reed. This park uses outdoor "rooms" to introduce children to horticulture through public art and hands-on exhibits.

Below right: Embarcadero Promenade
Designed by The Office of Michael Manwaring. These interpretive totems include poems and text on the cultural and natural history of San Francisco. They combine the role of street furniture with storytelling, creating an uncluttered but powerful environment.

Left and top left: The Blackstone River Valley National Heritage Corridor
Designed by Selbert Perkins Design. Heritage areas and parks can cover a few acres or hundreds of square miles, but whatever the size, their design development is similar, requiring a large number of distinct but simple pieces to be arranged to tell a story. Color, material, and detail must all be carefully planned to provide consistency over space and time.

Above and top right: Tyler Arboretum
Designed by Cloud Gehshan Associates. This simple interpretive panel provides a great deal of information on the surrounding environment, while also serving as a delicate piece of outdoor furniture.

Exhibition design for trade shows and showrooms

Designing exhibitions to sell products and services has grown into a hugely profitable industry. The level of design sophistication has also grown; trade show and showroom exhibitions have now become as detailed as other forms of exhibitions, to the point of becoming trendsetters for museums and traveling shows. This area of exhibition design has the most cross-fertilization of design professions with architects, event designers, trade show manufacturers, industrial designers, environmental graphic designers, and interior designers all contributing their skills, with the addition of the expertise of marketing strategists and sales representatives.

Trade show booth for Generali, Nationale Carrierebeurs 2006
Designed by TDM, Richard Schipper, and Veenstra Corporate. Italian hospitality, reliability, and tradition with an eye for the times in which we live: these are the topics on which the design of the Generali insurance company's trade fair stand is based. The red partition walls, on which the original Generali logo of 1831 is shown, combine modern and traditional aspects and place the emphasis on Italian hospitality. The trade fair stand can be put up and taken down at different locations and in different formats and dimensions again and again.

Trade shows

Trade shows present an organization's products and services. They are targeted at a specialized audience of purchasers and industry competitors. A few do engage the general public, but often hold a special early viewing for industry members only.

With numerous industries hosting events and a single venue having the capacity for hundreds or thousands of booths, trade shows are the most common type of exhibition design. Trade show designs focus on promoting a client's brand, hence it is critical to redesign the exhibition regularly in order to keep pace with changes in the company. Trade show design is fast-paced: it has the shortest deadlines of any type of exhibition in terms of design time, construction time, and life span. The process can be as short as two months for both design and build on a large-scale project. As deadlines are finite and predetermined, swift decisions need to be made, even if it means changing the design: if it's not ready in time, then there is no reason to have it.

The life span of these exhibitions depends on the client and the industry. A typical design can last between one and five years and its duration on the trade show floor is limited from three to five days either annually or several times a year in different locations. Exhibitions need to be adaptable and durable enough to be used at various shows, and appeal to different audiences. In contrast to museums, trade shows are market-driven, so the designs need to communicate the message to the audience very quickly and bluntly, and the amount of content is generally low.

In general, European trade fair exhibitions are designed by architects and are more spatially enclosed. The typical trade show designer in the US is an industrial designer who works at a design-build company that designs hundreds of trade show exhibits during the course of a year. Booths designed by these "exhibit houses" are generally designed as a kit or system of parts, and are usually limited to what the capabilities of their in-house shop can produce in a timely manner.

An independent design studio may design between one and 25 trade shows during the course of a year, and they will explore materials, design techniques, and experiential options that a single contractor may not be able to envision. The other advantage that an independent studio has is that their expertise is generally not limited to trade show design. Experiences in art, architecture, interior design, lighting, multimedia, and entertainment can make their way onto the trade show stage. Trade show design offers immense freedom for the creative designer. Trade shows allow for quick satisfaction for an environmental designer who otherwise would work on projects that take years to complete. Decisions and presentations must be made quickly in order to keep up with the fast-paced schedules. Clients are generally not involved with the design process, so it is critical for designers to understand and follow the brief.

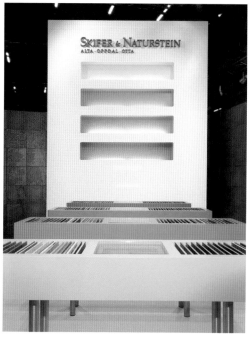

Trade show booths for Skifer & Naturstein (left and top) and Philips (bottom), traveling exhibitions

Designed by bachmann.kern & partner. European trade show booths are grand environments that often contain multiple levels, sometimes as freestanding buildings or as an occupant of an entire pavilion building where they can control the competition engagement. bachmann.kern & partner is a trendsetter in the creation of these stands using specialized furniture, lighting, and interactive objects to create exhibitions that simultaneously read as rooms, landmarks, billboards, and public spaces. The structures balance openness to attract potential customers with enclosure, to create a sense of privacy.

Above: Trade show booth for Pantone, NeoCon

Designed by Gensler. Gensler worked with Pantone on the idea that the company offers one color language for architecture and interiors, enabling designers and manufacturers to speak the same language to each other. Typical of most trade show exhibitions, Gensler had to work with a limited budget and efforts were made to keep expenses to a minimum. Furniture was borrowed from two manufacturers, the carpet was made by Pantone's partner, environmental graphics were produced in Chicago to avoid shipping costs, and the invitation and brochure were printed by Pantone's in-house printing division. The booth was treated in one color: pink.

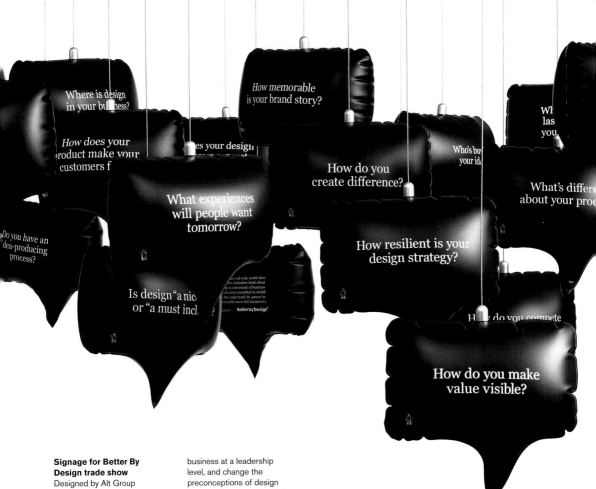

Signage for Better By Design trade show

Designed by Alt Group Limited. Not all trade show exhibitions are in a static box: some installations can drive the idea behind an entire show. Better by Design grew out of the New Zealand Design Taskforce strategy, which promotes the use of design as a differentiator for products and services in export markets. The challenge was to engage New Zealand business at a leadership level, and change the preconceptions of design being purely about aesthetics, rather than a fundamental business driver. This demanded a different approach, as images of design would only reinforce the status quo. The solution was to make "voices" visible using three-dimensional speech bubbles, containing provocative questions about the value of design.

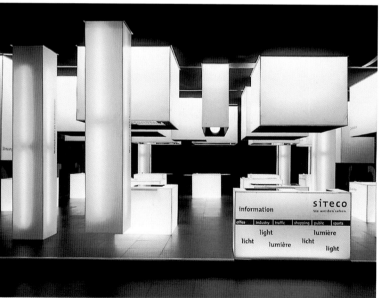

Trade show booths for Kodak, Photokina 2002 (above) and Siteco, Light & Building 2000 (left)
Designed by atelierbrückner. Color and light are direct ways of attracting attention on the trade show floor. These two exhibitions are bold and inviting at the same time. The giant cutouts used for the Kodak booth create a stage-like environment that encourages visitors to play with different points of view and perspectives. The lighting installation for Siteco was choreographed to produce a variety of lights and colors, altering the mood of the exhibition.

Showrooms

Like trade show exhibitions, showrooms are designed to display a company's products. Generally, they are not accessible to the general public unless they also function as retail environments, such as Apple's stores.

Showrooms are designed to last an average of one to five years at a permanent location, unlike trade shows which are in convention halls that change frequently. One of the most famous showroom venues is the Chicago Merchandise Mart. Thousands of contract furniture manufacturers showcase their products here all year round. The designer brings their clients to these showrooms generally by appointment only; it is not a casual drop-by situation as at a trade show. Showroom design occurs annually for NeoCon, an event held in Chicago for interior design professionals to see the latest products. Major manufacturers, such as Herman Miller, Knoll, Steelcase, and Haworth, present new showrooms to prove to the design community that they are the industry leaders. In Germany, center for the world's leading auto supply firms, showrooms are attached to corporate headquarters, with branded interiors seamlessly integrated with product exhibition. Italian and Japanese retail product showrooms are often located in jewel box buildings in major urban centers, a trend that is rapidly being adopted by the electronics and telecommunications industry.

Showrooms need to be designed with the utmost flexibility since all the exhibit properties—such as display cases, tables, and shelves—will be relocated or changed according to seasons and trends. The corporate marketing and design aesthetic for any given year evolves and will always require high visibility. Lighting plays a critical role in zoning out spaces, so it can help to make a space flexible.

Nolita & Ra-Re showroom, Bilbao
Designed by Arista diseño de espacios. This retail showroom uses experimental product display techniques.

Smart Car showroom, New York

Designed by Graham Hanson Design. This exhibition space for Smart Car uses the car itself as inspiration. The car is taken apart and put back together in multiple ways to describe aspects of the car, with simple text merely providing inspiration. The exhibition reaches a universal audience by creating its own object-based language.

Above: Teknion showrooms
Designed by Michael Vanderbyl. The design challenge for this showroom was to remedy the physical limitations of the space. The solution was to create an entrance compelling enough to draw visitors down a 20 foot (6m) long corridor to the soaring 17 foot (5m) tall showroom beyond–taking a negative and turning it into an advantage. The oval shape of the conference room helps to reduce the visual presence of this full-sized floating room, which also uses frosted glass panels to allow natural light to pass through the room and into the reception area.

Left: Tiles of Italy showroom, Milan Furniture Fair
Designed by Mitchell Mauk. The Milan Furniture Fair is Europe's leading showcase for the latest Italian furniture and home accessories. It takes place at the Milan Fairgrounds and is similar to a traditional trade show where the exhibits show for one week only. After this event, the space goes back to its usual flexible use. The combination of trade show and showroom space is an innovation that has come with the expansion of trade shows into million or more square foot spaces.

Apple Store, New York
Designed by Apple and
Bohlin Cywinski Jackson.
When Apple decided to open
the first Apple Store in New
York, its main goal was to
promote its brand and
cutting-edge products. Apple
proactively got involved in all
aspects of the design. The
store became a mecca for the
design community. The
sophisticated minimalist
approach was developed for
the first store and has been
used consistently in all
subsequent stores. Apple,
along with architect Bohlin
Czywinski Jackson, devised
an "art museum" approach to
showcasing products. The
store design has expanded
to include new products,
software, and accessories, as
well as a presentation theater
and a "Genius Bar," where
one can get help with any
product, software, or
hardware issue.

This page: Grammer AG showroom, Amberg

Designed by Wüstdesign. This auto supply showroom provides a powerful and forward thinking image by setting simple parts among brand imagery and interactive programs.

**Opposite page:
Mobitare AG, Suhr**

Designed by Designo AG. This in-store showroom uses flexible structures developed by the modular exhibition company Burkhart Leitner Constructiv to allow the creation and re-creation of displays very quickly. Light, object, and structure are delicately balanced in this display.

Traveling exhibitions

Almost since the beginning of exhibiting, shows have traveled. From displays of oddities which moved from town to town, to "blockbusters" organized by a major museum and then sent on the road to grand venues around the globe, these exhibitions have been designed to communicate in widely varying surroundings. More recently, an industry of traveling exhibitions has grown up to provide museums and other organizations with a relatively inexpensive and painless way to constantly refresh their offerings to their visitors. Both museums and for-profit commercial interests have undertaken to design, produce, manage, and rent out these peripatetic experiences,

thereby disseminating their intellectual and material riches to the world, and making money for themselves while doing it.

For the designer, traveling exhibitions pose a range of challenges. Most of these are practical and technical, and simply demand a full recognition of what sets these projects apart—namely, that they must repeatedly be packed up, loaded on a truck, unloaded, unpacked, set up, and broken down, and that all this should be achievable as easily and quickly as possible and with as little wear and tear to the exhibit itself. In reality, these requirements impact greatly on the design decisions that are made. A premium must be placed on

Benjamin Franklin: In Search of a Better World Designed by Staples & Charles. This exhibition appeared at six venues in the US and France. For Staples & Charles, the design of the project was an intellectual three-dimensional jigsaw puzzle, with continual questions of how best to convey Franklin, in all of his diversity, and how best to engage the visitor. This exhibition was a trendsetter for traveling shows, balancing objects with documents, media, and interactive pavilions. The show is also a marvel of demountability with large custom elements capable of being broken down into smaller pieces for travel. This is most evident in the Community "Junto" Tree, a fantasy in steel and fiber optics. It is designed in 16 sections that are assembled at each site.

specifying strong, durable, lightweight materials. Finishes must be especially robust, resistant to scuffs, scratches, and knocks. Connections between parts require particular attention: how many pieces do things break down into? How do you take them apart and put them back together over and over again? And the most important criteria of all: no single piece can be larger than the smallest door through which it must pass!

But it is not only construction considerations that demand attention. Questions of interpretation must be considered as well. Can fragile objects withstand the jostling and handling to which they will be subjected? What about the climate control fluctuations? Will mechanical and electronic interactives hold up over time? Will they require excessive maintenance, rebooting, and reprogramming? Will the venues supply the needed oversight, security, and repairs? Will adequate lighting be available everywhere, or should you consider the added expense and complexity of designing lighting into the exhibition itself?

Upper Branch

Lower Branch

Top Frame

Leaves

Protective Grill

Text

Institution
Symbols

Readerrail
Assembly

Text

1/2 of Tree Trunk Fins

6" High Round
Base Platform

9'-6" High central Core Assembly
Secured to the Base Platform

Readerrail & lower panels assembled in 2 units of 6 sections with 2 single
sections of removable service points. Base to be round, not faceted.

Darwin

Designed by the American Museum of Natural History. This exhibition started in New York before traveling to Boston, Toronto, and Chicago, before going to the Natural History Museum in London in time to celebrate the 200th anniversary of Charles Darwin's birth. To create a powerful mood within the confines of a traveling exhibition, the design refers to the Victorian context of Darwin's work, with dark wood and brass cases, while incorporating a contemporary perspective. It moves back and forth from an ordered rectilinear world with decorous Victorian detail for the sections focusing on Darwin's life, to curving organic shapes in the areas where discovery and science prevail. The section on the *Beagle* voyage is organized into little islands of content, and the pathway through the exhibition is evocative of the circuitous voyage itself. In contrast, the sections on Darwin's life in England are ordered into traditional rooms. The final section, on modern science, is defined by curved railings and graphic banners.

On the storytelling side, it must be noted that one can never be completely sure how an exhibition will be configured in each and every space in which it is installed. For this reason it is incumbent upon the designer to devise a flexible layout that can adapt to each venue. Linear narratives with a spatial sequence of a strong beginning, middle, and end can be difficult to deploy in some places. Thematic, or even random organizations, might be more adaptable.

Another characteristic associated with traveling exhibitions can come as a nasty surprise: they are usually much more expensive! Even a simple show composed of demountable graphic panels must bear the added cost of specialized materials and hardware, packing crates, transportation, insurance, etc. Just continue to multiply those costs as the scope and complexity of a project increases—special handling for objects and electronic equipment; complex installation processes; specialized structural and power systems; traveling work crews who are trained to install, break down, and maintain exhibits; duplicates for items that could break on the road; and added protection for all of it.

Today the subjects for traveling exhibitions are as broad and varied as are the stories out there to be told. Museums and other organizations have even reached out to a wider audience by creating "moveable museums" in vans and trucks, and the trend is only getting stronger.

Telling a story

As the work presented in this book shows, exhibition design spans a wide range of disciplines, but all exhibitions have one important thing in common; they all tell a story. Storytelling is the central craft of the exhibition designer, who creates a story from four elements: a narrative, a narrator, a path, and a context.

Narrative

When planning an exhibition, most institutions begin by determining the message that they wish to convey to their audience. However, by itself, this is not a story. The message only becomes a story when it is given a narrative thread with a clear beginning, middle, and end.

Narrator

A narrator is needed to drive the story forward. The narrator can be created using any number of mediums, such as text, graphics, or technology. Most exhibitions employ multiple narrative mediums.

Path

The path is what gives the story its structure, transforming the narrative into a three-dimensional space, which brings the story to life for each visitor. Just as in architectural and interior design disciplines, the space must be organized into a sequence that relates to the story and the visitors who will experience the exhibition. This sequence of experiences can be arranged around a timeline, theme, or hierarchy; any structure that has a consistent logic. Exhibitions provide this sequence of experiences in segments, building up the whole story, but never allowing the visitor to see the entire structure at once. Revealing the story step-by-step or through a series of possible steps is a key factor in engaging the visitor.

Context

Often the most neglected part of storytelling in exhibition design is the external context. An exhibition does not stand in a void, it is integrated into a building or landscape. How the visitor approaches and engages with the exhibition is as important as the exhibition itself. The visitor's introduction to the exhibition is not a part of the story, but is crucial to preparing the visitor for the experience.

Telling a story correctly

The primary role of an exhibition designer is to tell a story, but the obligation of a good exhibition designer is to use space, technology, displays, and materials effectively in service of that story. The following chapters focusing on the process and details behind exhibition development may seem daunting, but the designer is not alone: they have the support of multiple specialists throughout the process.

Left: Rock and Roll Hall of Fame
Architecture by Pei Cobb Freed & Partners, exhibition design by Pentagram. The Rock and Roll Hall of Fame building conveys a number of messages, from a sense of civic pride to the power of rock and roll. The building exterior supports the narrative of the exhibition inside it, as well as fulfilling a number of other roles, such as providing event space.

Above: The Freedom Trail, Boston
In exhibitions that utilize the environment, the path can be literal. The Freedom Trail is a line on the sidewalk that connects buildings which tell the story of the city's role in the American Revolution.

**_Petra: Lost City of Stone_,
traveling exhibition**
Developed by the American
Museum of Natural History.
This exhibition separates itself
from the surrounding space
by a gateway that mimics the
actual entrance to the rock
city of Petra. The gateway
establishes both the theme of
the exhibition and the actual
path of the narrative.

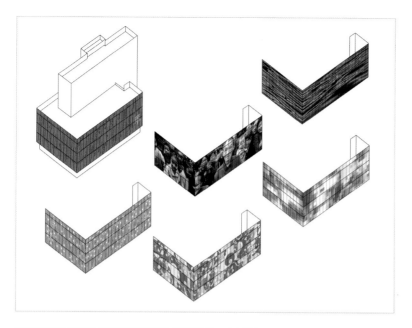

Building wrap, Jianianhua building, Chongqing
Designed by Skidmore, Owings & Merrill. Is it art, architecture, or exhibition design? This building wrap fulfills all the criteria of being an exhibition, using graphic panels to tell a story on a large scale. The Jianianhua building is the centerpiece of a retail and office complex in Chongqing, China. Using a standard triad signage system, the building's entire eight-story retail component becomes a slow-moving choreographed graphic.

Concept development

Initial concepts are often represented in a "napkin sketch" drawing where the designer's flash of inspiration is put down on paper, ready to be developed. The reality is that concept development is hard work, utilizing research, extensive planning, and ruthless editing. Concept development is where the elements that form the exhibition story take shape and direction.

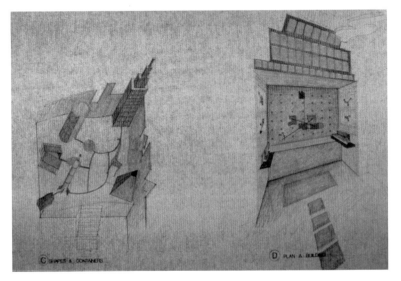

Napkin sketches
Designed by Lee Skolnick. The napkin sketch or parti drawing has its role in the concept development stage by bringing many ideas together in one drawing.

Below: Your Favorite Public Space exercise, 2006 Exhibition & Environment Design Symposium, Cranbrook Academy of Art
Led by Craig Johnson. This exercise focused on generating input that can lead to design ideas. Participants were asked to describe and analyze a favorite place, building, or exhibition.

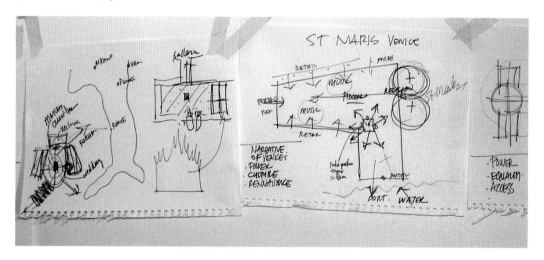

Left: Story creation exercise, 2006 Exhibition & Environment Design Symposium, Cranbrook Academy of Art
Led by Phil Hettema. This interactive exercise asked participants to visualize a fairy tale, providing a number of ideas about storytelling.

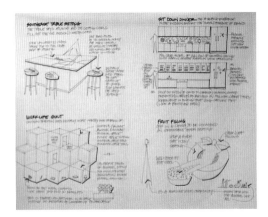

Sketchbook design process
Designed by Hellmuth, Obata + Kassebaum (HOK). Hal Kantner of HOK is an expert in a conceptualization process involving drawing concepts as they are developed by a group of stakeholders. These concepts are documented in a formal sketchbook, which is used to chart and refine ideas.

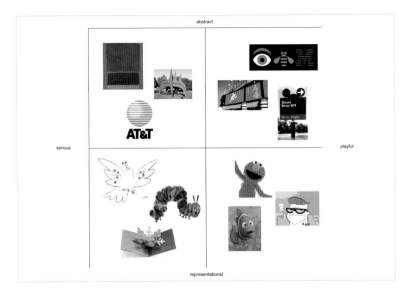

Managing expectations

The research phase consists of information accumulation and analysis. This period is not only when the designer accumulates knowledge of the client's needs and aspirations, but is also when the collaborative relationship between all the project stakeholders takes shape. This phase also includes setting the ground rules and expectations for the design process, including reconciling the project budget with the client's expectations.

Positioning diagram
The research and analysis stage in development can be enriched by the use of a number of approaches, including focus groups, brainstorming sessions, and positioning diagrams. The position diagram is an especially useful way of positioning a project against other sample projects in terms of budget and level of detail. All these devices are used to get a background of institutional needs and expectations before exploring design ideas.

More ideas

After all the research is accumulated comes the concept development stage. There are as many approaches to concept development as there are designers, with some firms building entire practices around this stage in the process. Whatever approach is taken, there are two practices that should always be employed by the designer: provide as many ideas as possible and explore a wide range of issues. This gives the designer credibility in the eyes of their client, by taking the design process in unexpected directions and by creating a vehicle for collaboration. This is the stage where lighting, material, and technology specialists can make the most impact on the final design, by bringing ideas to the table before they become too refined.

Distillation

After the rush of excitement in concept development comes the difficult process of distilling all of these ideas into two or five of the most powerful concepts. The final concept stage is only for the best ideas, not two opposing ideas: bad concepts have been approved this way! Concept documents at this stage also get refined into formal presentation documents and are reviewed using a "critique" process. If the concept survives this stage the designer can breathe a sigh of relief. The exhibition is ready for design development!

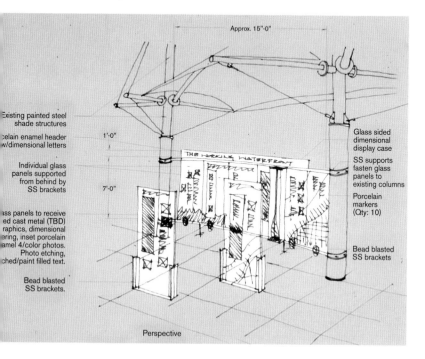

Hudson River Park interpretive master plan
Designed by Emphas!s Design. Documentation tightens up considerably when narrowing down final concepts. In this master plan, sketches were cleaned up from the research and concept development process for final presentation.

Approx. 15"-0"

Existing painted steel shade structures

celain enamel header w/dimensional letters

1'-0"

Individual glass panels supported from behind by SS brackets

7'-0"

ass panels to receive ed cast metal (TBD) raphics, dimensional ering, inset porcelain amel 4/color photos. Photo etching, ched/paint filled text.

Bead blasted SS brackets.

Glass sided dimensional display case

SS supports fasten glass panels to existing columns

Porcelain markers (Qty: 10)

Bead blasted SS brackets

Perspective

Design development

With an approved concept design in hand, the designer can proceed to the selection and development of the specific materials, colors, special equipment, and graphics that will further define the exhibition's character and enhance its interpretive power. Finishes, hardware, and other fabrication details are considered, though not necessarily specified yet. The nature and functioning of all interpretive and interactive exhibition components are fleshed out, pending more technical development in later phases. If lighting and acoustics have not been addressed yet, then they must be tackled now and at least preliminary schemes for their design must be prepared. Scripting for audio and video programs should be taking place and computer software development for controls and interactives should be in process.

Design development is also the time to test selected exhibition components, particularly mechanical interactives, through mock-ups and/or prototypes. Finally, a thorough budget analysis is critical at this point. Anything not explicitly included in this phase's budget will be an unwanted addition to the next cost estimate. If the designer's ideas are exceeding the client's cost parameters (not a rare occurrence), then some combination of scope reduction and/or design simplification needs to be arrived at. This is approached through a process commonly referred to as "value engineering," wherein the design and fabrication teams, along with the client, collaborate to find ways to fulfill as much of the stated mission, goals, and vision for the project within the agreed upon cost limits.

In general, it should be understood that the goal of the design development phase is to accomplish all decision making in anticipation of entering into the next phase—that of producing the actual construction and fabrication drawings and specifications—with as few remaining design questions as possible. At this point, the designer should be able to thoroughly envision the exhibition. Anything that appears hazy or undefined has not been designed sufficiently. The next phase should be about detailing, rather than designing.

Left: Memorial garden, Prince of Wales Hospital
Designed by Minale, Tattersfield, Bryce & Partners. In many cases the ideas are refined too a few very simple elements in design development. In this case, to convey the solemn nature of the story, this exhibition inside a hospital garden was limited to a few interpretive panels, coupled with plaques set on the ground.

Far left: *Good Grief!*, Children's Museum of Manhattan
Designed by the Children's Museum of Manhattan Exhibitions Department. In design development, the design team must value engineer the exhibition to meet the budget and best utilize in-house and outside resources. In this case, the design team faced the challenge of creating a highly interactive, three-dimensional world from the famous, two-dimensional comic strip. Sculptors created large-scale figures while in-house builders created such familiar landmarks as Snoopy's doghouse, Lucy's psychiatry booth, and Woodstock's nest. A large percentage of the budget was allocated to the figures to achieve the three-dimensional world effect.

Murano glass, Olnick Spanu Collection (above) and *Seaman Schepps: A Century of New York Jewlry Design 1904–2004*, Museum of Arts & Design (right)
Designed by Vignelli Associates. The exhibitions of Vignelli Associates are well noted for the way they are developed. Instead of creating a path to view the artwork, Vignelli Associates develop sculptural forms that can be viewed in detail or in their entirety. Display, object design, and interior effects are designed as a whole, instead of as a series of vignettes.

Materials

Selecting materials for exhibitions is like selecting materials for a house, only with more extremes at the low and high price ranges. An exhibition can be constructed for only a few dollars per square foot out of millwork and plastic, or for hundreds, even thousands, of dollars per square foot, out of stone, bronze, and glass.

Selecting materials is closely tied to the budget of the exhibition as well as its size and context. The most beautifully crafted exhibitions are trade shows and showrooms, where a combination of large budgets, small areas, and intense competition produce designs that use the best materials throughout. Even details such as furniture can be purpose made using expensive hard woods and metals. On the other extreme, the designers of temporary art shows are skilled at making inexpensive materials— such as vinyl print graphics, wallboard, and laminate—look chic and modern.

An all too common mistake is to choose materials solely to match the budget of a project. This can result in materials being used that are not durable enough to survive in high traffic areas or interactive exhibitions. At the same time, it makes little sense to use expensive materials in locations where the audience will not see them. The designer's role is to prioritize the quality of materials for the task of the exhibition, and to ensure the budget correctly reflects the material needs.

Finally, just as all materials are different, fabricators also have different levels of skill for handling materials. Stone, bronze, and glass require specialized craftsmen to detail and install. It makes little sense to spend the extra money on quality materials if they are not implemented successfully.

50 Books/50 Covers, AIGA headquarters
Designed by Chermayeff & Geismar. This exhibition was created from materials found in local hardware and lumber stores. A single table was made from standard table legs and "apple ply" stock, cut and varnished on site. The books are held in bookends secured to the edge of the table by clamps from a photography supply store. The inexpensive framing only enhances the quality of the books themselves.

Forbo Flooring showroom, Amsterdam
Designed by Concrete Architectural Associates. Prioritizing materials can create extreme contrasts. This showroom is anchored with three Möbius strips constructed out of durable steel and coated with Forbo's products. The background exhibition is constructed out of inexpensive, black MDF panels.

Media and technology

Integrating media and technology into exhibitions is a factor in the design process that can keep designers awake at night. Media technology is hugely expensive to install and has a voracious appetite for administrative time in planning and updating. However, media and interactive technology are indispensable in exhibition design today. There are now museums where constantly updated media is the central theme of the exhibition, and even the most conservative art galleries are using personal digital players and kiosks to augment their displays.

There are three important themes evident when selecting a media strategy: precedent, balance, and management.

Newseum
Designed by Ralph Appelbaum Associates. As the Newseum is devoted to portraying the news as it happens, the administration of content becomes just as important a design feature as the physical design.

Precedent is a powerful element in the selection of media technology. There are hundreds of new technologies available every year, but the design concepts behind many of these ideas have been around for years. Movies and media have been used effectively with slides, movies, television, and now LED and LCD screens. The medium may have changed, but the design approach stays the same.

A balanced presentation also plays a significant role in integrating media technology. With the cost of large-scale hardware dropping daily, it is easy to see a time when entire walls of an exhibition will consist of digitally changeable information.

However, traditional materials and display techniques will continue to be used to add balance to these environments.

The last major important design theme is content management and technical support. Media technology and content can go from being the most advanced feature of an exhibition to the most dated very quickly. This does not mean that hardware needs to be replaced every few years, but planned obsolescence should be a major feature of the original design, as well as being part of the operations plan for content updates.

The Deep
Designed by John Csáky Associates. Sound can play a crucial role in setting the mood for an exhibition, event, or individual displays. Localized sound through loudspeakers is used effectively in this aquarium. The exhibits also use plasma display panels, LCD projection screens, and interactive touch screens.

Lighting and acoustic design

When walking through an exhibition, do you ever ask yourself, "how do I feel?" Are you warm or cold, depressed, or annoyed when navigating an exhibition space? Most of these responses are affected by lighting and acoustics, often the most overlooked aspects of exhibition design, despite the crucial impact they have. Lighting and acoustics set the mood for a space, affect how objects will be displayed, and how information will be read.

Lighting is an especially controversial area in exhibition design because it reflects two differing design philosophies. Architects desire natural lighting in public spaces because this comforts visitors, while curators want to protect delicate objects and control the way they are viewed. The best exhibitions often use both natural and artificial light, using natural lighting to paint a broad picture and artificial light to focus on specific information. This balancing act has been made possible by of a number of technological advances, including new ways of combining natural light with theatrical lighting to create exciting spaces while still focusing on the preservation of artifacts,

and using the color temperature of accent lighting to create and manipulate moods based on crowd size. Improved lighting has led to better conservation of objects, with LED and fiber optic technology mitigating UV light and heat.

Acoustical issues face many of the same controversies as lighting, with the needs of noisy public circulation battling the desire for quiet spaces to view exhibition detail. Since exhibitions often sit inside large public spaces, moderating sound is crucial, whether it is in a large convention hall, a busy museum, or outdoors. The designer's role is not only to understand how sound establishes a mood and affects the narrative within an exhibition, but also to manage the transition between noisy public spaces and contemplative quiet areas. Acoustic design also has an operations element. The number of visitors flowing through the space at any one time is just as much a design decision as the physical structure of the exhibition. The administrative staff of the institution should be included in the acoustic design process. Their management of crowd flow has a crucial effect on acoustics.

Lighting and acoustics are yet more specialties that require extensive expert design collaboration. Specialists should be brought in early in a project, especially when the overall master plan for the exhibition is being developed. Since lighting and acoustics impact on everything from the size of the exhibition to the number of people that can attend, these decisions extend beyond surface design to affecting core business and content decisions.

Below: Ground Zero Viewing Wall
Designed by Pentagram. Light can serve as a creator of space. In this viewing wall at the former site of the World Trade Center in New York, the overhead light creates a small enclosure for reading the panels attached to the screen fence. At the same time, spot lighting in the open pit helps add definition to an environment that is in constant flux.

Right: *Frost*bite*, Sydney Opera House
Some exhibitions use an absence of light to create a mood. This exhibition hall has no windows and little natural light, but the decision was made to darken it rather than add light. The cream lino floor was covered in 3M self-adhesive vinyl, printed with monochrome images of letterpress type, and the white walls were sign-written with floor to ceiling letters reversed out in black. Multimedia displays and pinpoint lighting focused the viewer's attention on specific content.

Left: The Louvre Museum
The Louvre is one of the busiest museums in the world, with enormous public space requirements. A balance of natural and artificial light is used to separate public areas from gallery spaces. Interestingly, the museum receives the most natural light at underground and ground levels, with more subtly lit spaces in the upper reaches of the building.

Left and below: Hauserman showroom, New York
Designed by Vignelli Associates. These four shots show how different colored lighting can manipulate the mood of a space.

Trade show booths for Tatung (right) and Siegwerk (below)
Designed by bachman.kern & partner. Convention halls are noisy places where the general din of sound is ever present. Many successful exhibitions use subtle enclosures to create acoustic quiet zones while still leaving enough open space.

Exhibition design and the environment

Environmental sensitivity is becoming increasingly important to exhibition designers. With the development of institutions like the World Green Building Council and an increase in regulations, all designers are looking for materials and processes that are environmentally sensitive. Environmental sustainability is of the greatest importance to exhibition designers because of the materials they have to work with. The hot and bright lights used in most exhibitions are an enormous energy drain, plus large amounts of energy are involved in moving large-scale exhibitions. The printing and etching of information graphics often uses harmful and difficult-to-dispose of chemicals.

Exhibition designers are using three approaches to achieve sustainability: decreasing energy consumption, using recyclable materials, and decreasing the use of harmful chemicals. Selecting materials and processes may seem easy on the surface, as more and more eco products are available, but this is deceptive. Often the materials that are the most harmful are also the most necessary to the success of the exhibition, and institutions and designers alike are often loath to sacrifice aesthetics for sustainability.

The key to environmental sustainability is designing for the life span of an exhibition. Degradable materials may work well for a temporary show meant to last only a couple of months in one location, but may not hold up to the rigors of a traveling show or an outdoor exhibition. High-energy lighting is not as large an issue for a small-scale trade show exhibition as it is for an entire museum.

Sustainability strategy works best when it is integrated early into the design process. Many design firms integrate environmental strategy into the storyline of the exhibition, making the sustainable nature of the materials used transparent to the audience. This is most evident in corporate exhibitions and trade shows, where the company's commitment to the environment can be a central storyline. Making sustainability part of the story also makes the balancing act between the environment and durability over time more apparent when key design decisions are being made.

Trade show booth for Prana, traveling exhibition

Designed by Gensler. Prana is an environmentally active company, and this trade show set the tone for a future retail store design by utilizing green building techniques and sustainable materials. The booth needed to use durable materials to withstand repeated set-up and transport to multiple venues. A complete environmental strategy was developed, from the use of compact fluorescent lighting to using hemp rope to create a soft barrier for the exhibition. Nearly the entire exhibition is recyclable, including its metal shipping container.

Pierce County Environmental Services building

Panels designed by AldrichPears Associates. This building incorporates sustainable design elements such as light wells, natural air circulation, and roof water collection. The site, an old gravel mine overlooking Puget Sound, is being reclaimed through a 50-year master plan, which will incorporate a wastewater treatment plant and will replace the mine with recreational facilities and an environmental education center. AldrichPears designed the interpretative panels that explain the Environmental Services' vision and the site's history and geology, as well as issues such as graywater reclamation, landscaping, and erosion control. Visitors are given an inside look into this often unseen world, and take away a sense of personal relevance and responsibility for the environment. By integrating sustainability into this exhibition, the green aspects of the building are made transparent.

Neue Raeme, traveling exhibition

Designed by Stefan Zwicky. One of the leading approaches to creating more sustainable traveling exhibitions is to use lightweight, modular materials. These materials are cheaper to transport, use less energy in their construction, and are easier to recycle. This design uses fabric and modular steel rods to create a light, but expansive environment.

Storytelling and documentation

Documenting a story in exhibition design offers endless possibilities as well as pitfalls. Since exhibition designers come from so many different professional groups, each with their own approaches and styles, the documentation employed must be accessible to all of these groups, serving as the key communication device throughout the concept development, design development, fabrication, and management process.

Concept documents

There are as many concept document approaches as there are concepts, from physical and computer models to storyboards and sketches that show how exhibitions are to be navigated and experienced. No matter what the drawing type employed, it is important that drawings made at the conceptual level are produced at the most professional level possible. Concept drawings are often duplicated widely and used in a variety of ways, including as visuals for stakeholder meetings, as fundraising documents, and as marketing materials. The other important aspect of concept documents is clarity. Since the final exhibition will probably look very different from the concept documents, the central themes and ideas behind the story must remain clear and serve as a guide for the exhibition.

Documentation for WordSpring Discovery Center
Designed by Lorenc+Yoo. In a single project, designers can use dozens of different documentation approaches starting with storyboards and then proceeding to explore the exhibition in sections and through models, finally ending with shop drawings and prototypes.

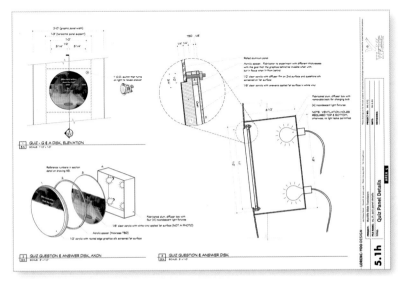

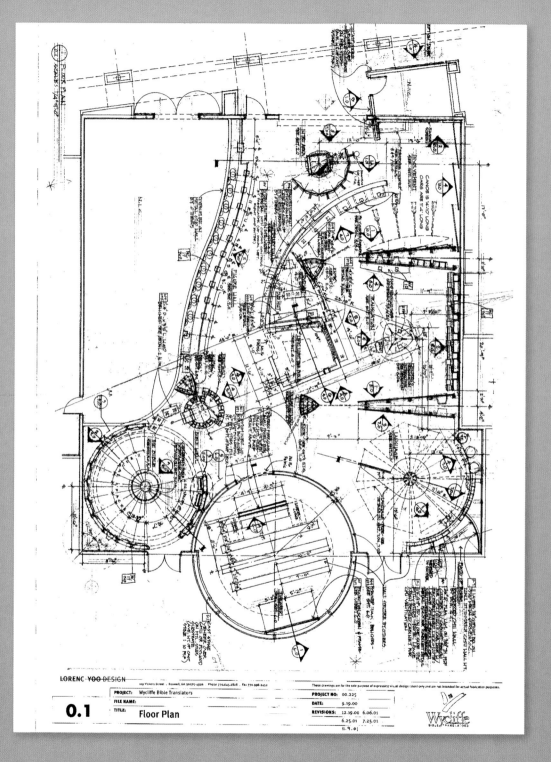

LORENC · YOO DESIGN

PROJECT:	Wycliffe Bible Translators
FILE NAME:	
TITLE:	Floor Plan

0.1

These drawings are for the sole purpose of expressing visual design intent only and are not intended for actual fabrication purposes.

PROJECT NO:	00.225
DATE:	9.19.00
REVISIONS:	12.19.00 6.06.01
	6.25.01 7.25.01
	11.9.01

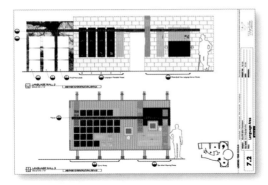

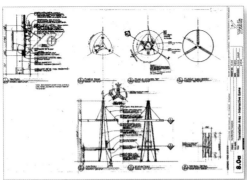

Design intent documentation

Design intent documentation is often confused with construction documentation in which every design detail is spelled out through drawings. Since exhibition design can be an exciting collaboration between designers and fabricators, design intent documents are in fact a collaborative communication medium for explaining how a designer would like their exhibition to look to the myriad experts and fabricators involved in the process. Though design intent documents can take on many levels of detail, including text, the two most crucial aspects that must be included are scale and material specification. With an understanding of these two areas, a designer from nearly any field can communicate their vision. The most important skill a designer needs is not documentation knowledge, but confidence in their ability to communicate intent.

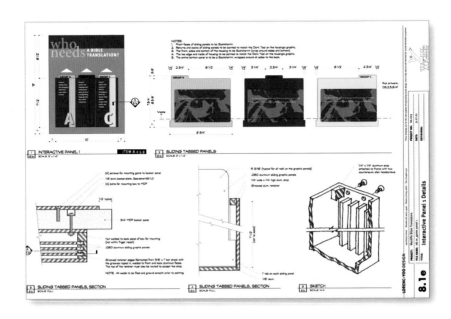

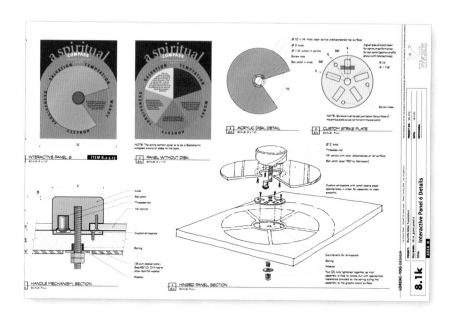

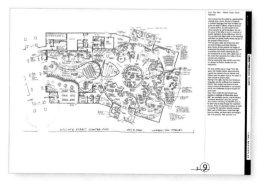

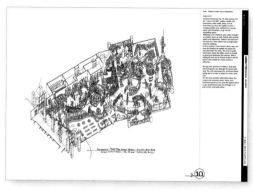

Shop drawings, as-builts, prototypes, and photographs

One of the most exciting aspects of documenting an exhibition is working with a fabricator. Since a fabricator's role is to visualize the actual exhibition in the specific way it will be built, they use a number of tools to communicate with the designer and client. Chief among them are shop drawings and as-builts; documents that detail the exhibition elements as closely as possible. Often drawings are not enough to visualize how a display will be put together. In these cases, fabricators may document prototypes of exhibition details. This reliance on fabricator direction may seem like a scary lack of control for many designers, but this is in fact how the best architects and designers worked, including Frank Lloyd Wright and Carlo Scarpa.

Design standards

Upon completion of an exhibition design, a set of documented standards are often needed to ensure that the exhibition is maintained at a high quality. Some exhibitions, such as heritage parks and art exhibitions, have standards that must be administered over long periods of time by many different designers. Trade shows and traveling shows require extensive instructions for erection and dismantling. Documentation of standards is put into a design manual that not only contains the design elements, but also standards for how the story must be told and new additions made. The standards manual represents the culture of the institution and how it sees its identity through exhibition.

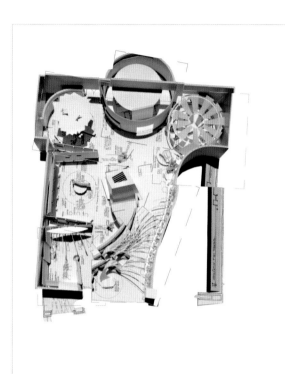

Progress in Design - Phase 2 Schematic Design

This document represents 100% submittal for the schematic design outlining the spaces, the features, the spaces for graphics, and A/V and lighting.

This has been a collaboration with Frank Campbell (HBPM) and their engineers to inform of any architectural requirements. It has included Bill Platt as A/V, lighting and acoustic consultant.

The model to the left is the culmination of this design which has in turn produced a set of drawings (see section 6) and these have been used for "ballpark" construction pricing estimates by both Designers Workshop and Bill Platt (see section 10).

This phase has produced a platform for the next phase of work in Phase 3 DD.

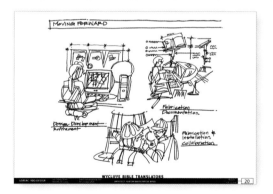

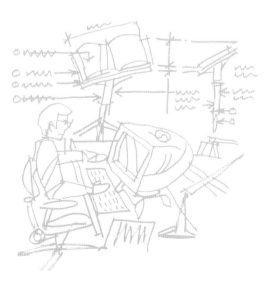

Choosing a fabricator

If you have read the book this far, you have probably come to the conclusion that being an exhibition designer takes equal parts ego (to fulfill your vision) and humility (to seek the support of the people who will be carrying out that vision). No area of exhibition design requires this combination of traits more than selecting and working with a fabricator. The outcome of the finished product is what will be remembered—not just the beautiful design on paper—and it is the goal of the fabricator to achieve that intent in physical form. The key to any successful relationship requires not just a shared vision, but also an understanding of each other's talents. The selection of a fabricator starts with mutual respect, and that trait will be evident in many ways throughout the process. Factors to consider when choosing a fabricator include: quality of past work, open-mindedness to new technologies and approaches, a background in experimentation, an understanding of project pricing, capabilities of specialized crafts, and experience of working with different designer personalities.

With so many factors to consider choosing a short list of fabricators can take a long period of time. Designers typically choose between three and five fabricators to bid, depending on how big the job is and how much time they want to spend visiting shops and interviewing senior staff. Many designers too often over-prepare documents for bidding. A good design bid package should have enough information to communicate the design approach, equipment, materials, and dimensions, but does not need to spell out every fabrication detail. The designer must trust that an experienced fabricator will use their own extensive experience to develop approaches that the designer may have missed. Building a greater understanding of background and experience will come from follow-up conversations to learn how the contractor came up with their bids. This step will uncover if the fabricator understands the designer's intent. A good fabricator may suggest materials or approaches that will lower prices, while suggesting that other areas may require even higher levels of detailing than the designer originally specified.

Fabricator selection sounds particularly onerous and time consuming, but the process gets much easier with time and experience. Some designers have built up such a solid relationship with fabricators that they are brought in as consultants early in the design concept stage. This trend will only grow with time as many clients are demanding more design build services, as well as trying to get a handle on costs during initial planning.

The Saudi Aramco Exhibit Center

Designed by West Office Exhibition Design, fabricated by Design Craftsmen. One key factor in selecting a fabricator is their ability to deliver and implement exhibitions in other countries. In this case, the fabricator needed to ship the exhibition in parts over 7,000 miles from the US to Saudi Arabia, receive all the necessary permits, and assemble and test the exhibition. Globalism has affected the exhibition design industry greatly, with a number of companies, especially in the trade show and showroom arena, able to service worldwide clients.

Evaluation

Evaluation is the tool for designers to learn what is effective and what is not in design. A designer may think they know what makes an exhibition work with an audience, but in reality, the complexity of weighing the goals of the stakeholders and audience make objective evaluation important.

Pre-evaluation or proof of concept

The pre-evaluation stage is the most creative part of the evaluation process, where concepts and storylines are developed from a range of ideas. This is the stage where the exhibition audience and goals are determined. Designers and evaluators work in close contact, and many institutions and design firms have built their practices around their own specialized approaches. The pre-evaluation stage is also the phase where many new design strategy approaches are developed. Today, more evaluations include experience evaluation, which analyzes the behaviors of people to determine what exhibitions may work best instead of segregating audiences by demographics. There are also efforts to integrate corporate or institutional branding into the evaluation process. These efforts determine what exhibition design approach may work best, not just for the narrative, but also for the overall identity of the institution. This approach is especially important in the area of donor recognition, where contributor credit must be skillfully integrated into the overall exhibition story.

Prototype testing for Discover Philadelphia
Signage design by Cloud Gehshan. Before the rollout of 300 signs in Philadelphia, an interpretive sign system prototype was developed that matched how the final object would appear for one final evaluation.

Five Friends from Japan, traveling exhibition
Designed by Cambridge Seven Associates, Inc. and John Heyward People, Place and Design Research. This exhibition shows the lives of five Japanese children by presenting a typical Japanese classroom and five different home and family settings. The exhibition's goals are to foster awareness and understanding among American children of people from other cultures and provide compelling exhibition experiences on Japanese culture. The researcher on this project coordinated activities closely with the design team from the initial exhibit conceptualization, and helped establish many ideas, including having a distinctly modern sophisticated Japanese sensibility.

Mock-ups and prototypes or formative evaluation

Mock-ups and prototypes are a great way of testing audience reactions. Mock-ups are rough design ideas made to test the audience's reactions to specific design details. Mock-ups can be modeled out of inexpensive materials such as clay, paper, foam, or any extra scraps of material. The purpose is to hash out how an exhibition may be constructed and provide an extra visual study aid. The more mock-ups tested in various conditions, the more successful and accurate a study. Prototypes are much more elaborate mock-ups, which try to duplicate real-world conditions as much as possible. This may mean building part of an exhibition out of actual materials used in the final fabrication. Prototype evaluation gives the most realistic portrayal of the design and serves usually as the last chance to make any changes.

Post-evaluation or summative evaluation

Post-evaluation is conducted after an exhibition is completed. Post-occupancy tests often switch from the highly controlled testing that precedes it, to a more hands-off observational approach. Observational tests can include timing the visitor as they navigate the exhibitions, observing their path throughout the space, and studying their interactions with exhibitions. Analysts may offer surveys of audience reactions to the exhibition as a whole. In many cases, post-occupancy tests are dropped from the design program, usually because of a lack of budget, or a lack of desire to point out mistakes at the end of a long process. This is a big mistake. Exhibitions do not exist in a vacuum, but are part of ongoing institutions that will be adding and changing exhibitions over time. In the case of traveling exhibitions, like trade shows, post-evaluation testing must occur many times, to hone the effectiveness of the presentation for successive audiences.

Who should do the design evaluation?

There is much debate about who should be conducting design evaluation. Designers often believe they are the best judges of how their designs can be used and conduct their own analysis without outside assistance. The reality though is that even the most objective designers have a difficult time providing thorough evaluation, especially in the middle of the design process. No matter how experienced the designer, no one is perfect and everyone has limited vantage points. Outside evaluation gives that unbiased point of view that helps widen the perspective on a design. Exhibition evaluators are a distinct professional subgroup that specialize in areas ranging from museum exhibitions to trade shows. Their role is to partner with clients and designers throughout the design and implementation process, providing guidance on audience needs.

Above: Trade show booth for Formica, NeoCon

Designed by Kuhlmann Leavitt, Inc. Cindy Adams, a specialist in trade show and display analysis, has research that shows that the most effective trade show booths are often the ones with the highest design standards for detail and quality. Effective trade show attributes include strong attention-getting devices, good use of materials, and an ability to draw people into the space. Sales force training and advanced tracking procedures also enhance the effectiveness of the display. This booth exemplifies these traits. It uses light to draw visitors in, and then surrounds them with high quality flooring and sharply detailed furniture. While the booth is inexpensive both in initial construction and operation cost, high-quality materials are put to the most effective use.

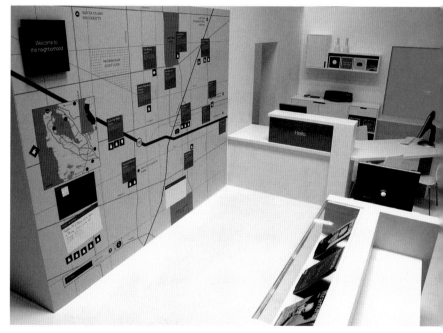

Above: Exhibition for TownePlace Suites

Designed by IDEO. The TownePlace Suites are hotels for long-term visitors. They do not try to emulate home life, as is often the model for hotels, but instead provide information on a number of opportunities available to hotel residents looking for excitement in a new city. This exhibition in the lobby of a hotel was developed around an experience analysis of guest behaviors, which involved observing and interviewing hotel guests. IDEO's evaluation resulted in radically different design ideas and models.

Portfolios

The work collected here represents the diversity of contemporary exhibition design. One important group that is covered elsewhere in this book, but not in this section, is the work of in-house museum facilities, corporations, and institutions, which can be every bit as strong as the work of private firms. Examples include the wonderful display work of IKEA and Apple, and Ellen Lupton's cutting-edge exhibition work for the Cooper-Hewitt National Design Museum. But the goal of selecting these particular portfolios is to showcase design processes and approaches across numerous design projects.

These companies represent a phenomenon occurring in exhibition design in the last few decades: the integration of exhibition design work between in-house design teams and design firms with multiple clients and projects. This has created a world of practice with both institutions and independent firms providing design leadership. The design firms and in-house designers feed off the creativity of each other to make more and more exciting design work that develops and enriches the environment.

Large-scale museums and institutions have also taken a leadership role. The Chicago Museum of Science and Industry has a design team of 40 members undertaking an ambitious group of exhibitions yearly, while at the same time collaborating on projects with a diverse group of design firms such as Hettema Design and Gallagher Associates.

The design firms represented here were selected in part based on their desire to break traditional boundaries in the way exhibitions are designed and implemented. Their work spans architecture, landscape, interiors, art, graphics, and technology to tell stories and develop integrated narratives. The work presented also shows design diversity from small-scale displays to large-scale environments. In exhibition design, there is no such thing as a standard project. These design firms may be asked to create a book, a single exhibit, an entire exhibition, a building, or even the ongoing master plan for an institution.

The firms also represent another trend: the globalization of design. Agencies like Pentagram and Ralph Appelbaum Associates have become brand name firms around the world, while companies from Australia to Germany are collaborating on projects in Asia. At the same time, a limited talent pool has created international design centers. It is no accident that most of the firms exhibited here reside in New York, London, Frankfurt, Sydney, Seoul, and Beijing. These cities are rapidly becoming international capitals of design.

Atelier Markgraph

The architectural writer Conway Lloyd Morgan provides perhaps the best description of Frankfurt-based design company Atelier Markgraph in his book on the firm: "For decades, museums and trade shows remained separate. Atelier Markgraph is one of the pioneer firms to bring museum-level exhibition design process to large-scale exhibitions." The firm is a leader in the exhibition as spectacle, engaging large groups and even entire cities, in the storytelling process.

Atelier Markgraph's work extends beyond the three-dimensional, using light and movement as central components of its designs. The spaces themselves seem simple and stark, using dynamic elements to enliven them and interact with audiences. Utilizing light and technology allows Atelier Markgraph to expand its exhibitions to the size of a city or an arena while still providing an intimate connection between the audience and the space.

The firm uses jaw-dropping spectacle and advanced technology to promote and further the story behind its work, including lasers, fiber optics, and mipex (specialized LED modules). To achieve these effects, Atelier Markgraph employs lighting designers and technology specialists in the same interdisplicinary teams as designers and strategists. The results are spaces and exhibitions that are dramatic, but tightly focused around the specific story and themes. Atelier Markgraph focuses on production early in the design process. Since many of these exhibitions are on an enormous scale, but are also impermanent, the erection and dismantling of the environments are developed early in the design process. This results in exhibitions that are modularized in complex ways, with distinct connections between technology, print graphics, and display objects.

Far right: DaimlerChrysler, IAA 2005
Right: DaimlerChrysler, Expo 2000
These exhibitions for Mercedes-Benz (see next page) and DaimlerChrysler typify the large scale, yet focused spaces Atelier

Markgraph designs for corporate exhibitions. The DaimlerChrysler exhibitions use interactivity to engage the visitor, using light projectors to create excitement in the audience before they view the cars.

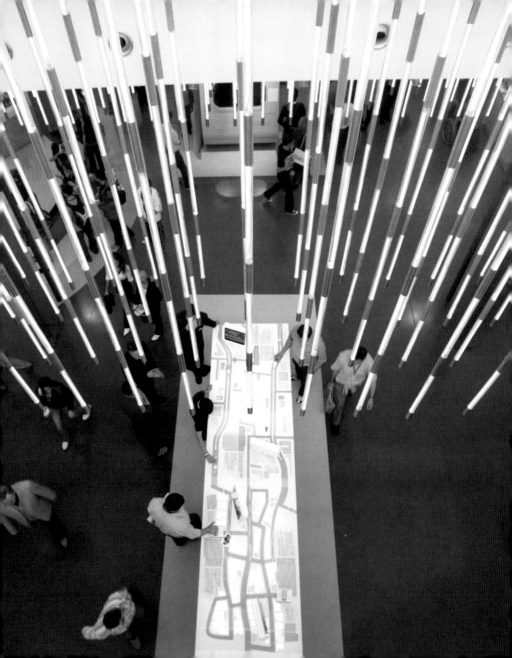

Above: Mercedes-Benz, IAA 2003
Right and far right: Mercedes-Benz, IAA 2005

The Mercedes-Benz 2003 exhibition centers around a "floating" ring shape. The shutter-blind facade contained LED strips which, together with a screen, anchored the technology themes into the large space. The 2005 exhibition focused around the power of the cars themselves, using lighting and the sweeping space to engage the audience.

Above: *ILLUMINATION: EVOLUTION*, **Senckenberg Natural History Museum** Opposite, top: *The Frankfurt Sound*, **Institut für Stadtgeschichte** Opposite, bottom: *The King Makers*, **various locations**
For museum exhibitions, Atelier Markgraph focus on using light and interactive staging to engage the audience. For the Frankfurt light culture festival Luminale 2004, the Senckenberg Natural History Museum showcased its natural history treasures in a new light. Featuring video installations, light, and sound design *ILLUMINATION: EVOLUTION* guides visitors through four billion years of evolution. *The King Makers* exhibition was spread across four different museums in Frankfurt, involving a subtle and balanced use of light accents for the existing sights being profiled. For *The Frankfort Sound*, projected and moving light images flow through tableaus that reflect on the history of jazz.

ON AIR

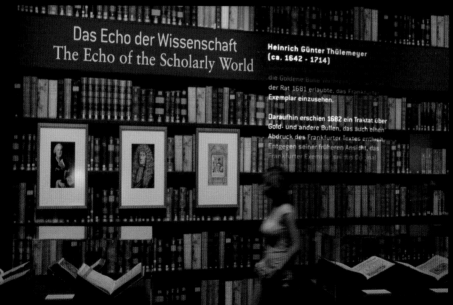

Das Echo der Wissenschaft
The Echo of the Scholarly World

**Heinrich Günter Thülemeyer
(ca. 1642 - 1714)**

die Goldene Bulle verlegt.
der Rat 1681 erlaubte, das Frankfurter
Exemplar einzusehen.

Daraufhin erschien 1682 ein Traktat über
Gold- und andere Bullen, das auch einen
Abdruck des Frankfurter Textes enthielt.
Entgegen seiner früheren Ansicht, das
Frankfurter Exemplar sei das Original

Opposite: Future Zone, T-Online Experience Center, Darmstadt

How do you show the future? The main aim of the T-Online Experience Center in Darmstadt was to give audiences an interactive, three-dimensional experience of the future of communication, based on tomorrow's products, services, and technology. Inside the 984 square foot (300m²) Future Zone at T-Online's headquarters, visitors travel through time to learn how online communication is evolving. The exhibition is structured across two rooms, the first room sets the mood for the corporate image of T-Online. Room two provides an experience of the future: the Best Online Experience where visitors are led to the walk-through "T-Online Browser," which offers a three-dimensional immersion in the world of T-Online products and services.

Top right: KUNST|RAD (ART|WHEEL), Museum Riverbank Festival
Right: SkyArena, 2006 FIFA World Cup

Working on the scale of a city, these two projects use sheer spectacle to communicate. For the 2005 Frankfurt Museum Riverbank Festival, a ferris wheel became a stage for the city's museums. Each museum had its own gondola, which had a specific theme. Projections from the gondola exhibitions were then projected on a large screen that made up the center of the wheel. The wheel is capable of changing themes for different events. For the 2006 FIFA World Cup, a sound and light show in Frankfurt illustrated World Cup history on a city scale.

Lee H. Skolnick Architecture + Design Partnership

Established in 1980 in New York, Lee H. Skolnick Architecture + Design Partnership (LHSA+DP) stands at the intersection of architecture and interpretation. Founder and Lead Designer Lee H. Skolnick, FAIA, has dedicated his professional life to exploring the ability of design to function as an interpretive tool, connecting people to their culture and communities, in particular, through mining the inherent narrative which lies within every situation. To that end, the firm has created a process of thoughtful and sensitive development of content and design with the visitor in mind, focusing its efforts on attracting diverse audiences and learning styles, and fostering intergenerational learning.

By understanding the specific needs of each project and its targeted audiences, LHSA+DP works to create "personal entry points" and interpretive opportunities through the designed experience, empowering the visitor to make connections between the content, their personal interests, and their everyday lives. Understanding the audience's preconceived notions, base knowledge levels, and genuine curiosity and interest in the themes and artifacts is paramount to creating meaningful and memorable visitor experiences. The resulting work is immersive with the form of the display, the path through the environment, and the design of the information providing entry to the deeper educational content.

To achieve this, the firm consciously blurs the lines between various design disciplines, using a multi/interdisciplinary approach to create the best solutions for each project. The ability to create an entire building from the ground up or understand the implications of an existing building space—the firm is also accomplished in residential and commercial architecture—is reflected in the creation of spaces that can function and communicate on a number of levels. Some of LHSA+DP's exhibits are integrated in workplaces and educational centers, creating dynamic working environments as well as educational exhibits.

The National Track & Field Hall of Fame

LHSA+DP's work for The National Track & Field Hall of Fame uses a variety of media and technologies–including projection and touch screens–to bring the history, physiology, health benefits, and technologies of track and field to life for an intergenerational audience. The Hall of Fame exhibits are seamlessly incorporated into the activities of an existing building: a track and field center that hosts events throughout the year.

Miami Children's Museum
Of particular significance in the work of LHSA+DP has been the opportunity to design engaging and educational children's museum environments. The Miami Children's Museum aims to encourage multicultural awareness and appreciation in visitors aged 0–10 and their families through the themes of Culture, Community, and Communication. Using a variety of techniques, such as immersive environments, hands-on interactives, multimedia, and creative and imaginative play, visitors explore homes, neighborhoods, and the world beyond.

Children's Museum of the East End (CMEE)

CMEE encourages visitors aged from three months to 12 years, and their families, to explore the world around them through the theme of a "journey" into the familiar and the unknown, the real and the imagined, the natural and the urban. Using a variety of techniques including dioramic displays, interactive screens, and sculptural objects, visitors learn about local and natural history through immersive environments including a magical bedroom, a tree house, a village store, a potato chip factory, a musical forest, a fishing boat, and many more. Extensive site planning and landscape design features were also utilized to create an environment where a broad range of outdoor activities can take place.

**Sony Wonder
Technology Lab**

The design concept for this
corporate exhibition was to
merge education,
entertainment, and technology
into an interactive experience
which encourages visitors to
use creative expression while
engaging in innovative and
digital technologies. Sony's
emphasis on creating a
networked digital environment
world with limitless access
to content led to a design
vocabulary emphasizing
fluidity, connectivity,
and personalization.

**Off the Wall,
AIGA headquarters**
This low-budget exhibition is a collaboration between LHSA+DP, the Society for Environmental Graphic Design (SEGD), and the American Institute of Graphic Arts (AIGA). *Off the Wall* invites visitors to experience dimensions of communications and information, wayfinding and signs, identity and environments, and interpretive exhibits and retail. As visitors approach the storefront gallery, they notice letters forming the title of the exhibition transforming from two dimensions to three dimensions on the surface of the glass. This device attempted to lay the conceptual groundwork for the installation—the idea of graphics and design moving from a two-dimensional plane to a three-dimensional environment. The rear gallery space presented a dialogue between designers and the general public. A series of six translucent monoliths contained statements by designers on the meaning and impact of environmental graphic design.

Lorenc+Yoo Design

Atlanta-based Lorenc+Yoo Design (LYD) boasts a broad skill set, specializing in what it terms "environmental communication design," an encompassing genre that includes exhibits, signage, retail spaces, furniture, and graphics. According to company Principal Jan Lorenc, a passion for crafting a good story is the key to the firm's success: "We are storytellers and the narrative is the environment we create. We encourage institutions and companies to convey a tangible message through the use of images, words, and film. Together, these media contribute to a broad and complete narrative environment that tells a story better than words and images alone."

LYD's work is typically coordinated with a team of architects, interior designers, landscape architects, and marketing professionals, working both inside and outside the firm. The creative process remains the same regardless of the particular job; its basis is a holistic investigation into the client's organization, seeking to uncover its individual story and express it in a coherent and attractive manner. "Our approach looks at the company or environment and strives to incorporate the richness of its culture and context into the project," says Lorenc. "Everything from the site plan, to the landscape, lighting, building, interiors, and graphic images...everything down to the micro level is part of the unified and unique narrative."

LYD's design process is drawing-intensive, and uses multiple analysis and documentation approaches. This multifaceted approach ensures that all project stakeholders are fully engaged and contribute to the unified story being developed. A project may include storyboards, a design element matrix, a planning analysis, and a written narrative. Throughout the design process, this story becomes more refined and developed as individual design specialists add their expertise. Despite the high level of collaboration, the project designer maintains the leading role, making sure that the message is consistently articulated from the macro to the micro level.

LYD focuses on integrating dynamic technology into the storytelling process, such as simple passive screens or more complex interactive devices. The desire for movement and an ability to tell an ongoing story is crucial to creating rich interpretive environments and dynamic media is integrated into nearly every exhibition, with content management an integral part of the design process.

Theater entrance, Mayo Clinic Heritage Hall
The theater shows orientation and other films highlighting the values of the Mayo Clinic. The design of the entrance honors the clinic's architectural heritage using the 1912 cornerstone from the original Mayo Clinic building, stained glass, and a ceiling light from the 1928 Plummer building, and Italian marble that complements the 2001 Gonda building. The stained glass portal creates a welcoming light to guide visitors into the theater.

...half-opened door *into the future*, full of interest, *intriguing*, beyond my power to describe...

William J. Mayo, M.D.
1935

1912

WordSpring Discovery Center

This center is dedicated to the work of Wycliffe–an organization whose aim is to translate the Bible into all the languages of the world. This 4,500 square foot (1,370m^2) museum houses a theater and interactive displays that showcase the process of translation and highlight some of the languages and cultures that Wycliffe has worked with. The design of the center uses multiple materials to represent the different cultures where translation occurs.

Above: Georgia-Pacific distribution center

This corporate exhibit space tells a three-part story about the processes, products, and customers of the Georgia-Pacific manufacturing company. Located in a vast space in the distribution center, the sculptural forms had to match the scale of their surroundings. A tape measure doubles as a timeline that becomes a cyclone connecting the different narrative sections. This work is indicative of LYD's corporate and trade show projects, which break free of the confined space and clutter of the show floor to create immersive, welcoming environments for visitors.

Right: Mayo Clinic Heritage Hall

The Mayo Clinic Heritage Hall is a 4,000 square foot (1,220m²) visitor center that acknowledges the contributions of major benefactors to the clinic's success. It includes exhibits on the clinic's benefactors, trustees, and founders.

**Left: Trade show booth
for Related Urban
Development, ICSC 2005**
Designed for the ICSC
convention in Las Vegas, the
Related Urban Development
exhibit employed a bold brand
identity for the company. In
reflecting the company's
values of stable yet
progressive real estate
development, LYD chose a
rich, modern visual vocabulary
of understated planes set at
angles, and translucent
frosted white acrylic walls to
create a combined sense of
monumentality, elegance,
and excitement.

**Left: Zamias/First Union
trade show booth**
This design is inspired by an
agora, a Greek marketplace,
presenting Zamias Services
as a company firmly grounded
in tradition but with its eye
squarely focused on the
future. This "modern-classic"
theme gives visitors the
impression of walking through
a marketplace, surrounded by
display windows filled with
items for sale, while a
graphic wall frieze tells
the company's story.

Top: Sony-Ericsson brand launch, CTIA
The joining of forces of Sony and Ericsson, two giants in the fields of electronics and telecommunications, required a highly visible exhibition structure. This simple white booth stood out elegantly amid the visually hyperactive displays nearby. In order to set the booth apart even more, LYD incorporated two-story "S" and "E" letters—for Sony Ericsson—to serve as the dominant design feature.

Above and above left: Haworth showroom, Chicago
Haworth asked LYD to redesign their existing 24,000 square foot (7,315m²) showroom space to complement product display and establish a bold identity expressing the company's vision, core values, and key "stories." Space, words, and images work together to literally surround Haworth's products and customers with a comfortable and compelling atmosphere. LYD worked closely with the Haworth team to create a visually dynamic environment that communicates company goals on a variety of levels, while solving pragmatic constraints of time, space, and cost effectiveness.

Mauk Design

Mauk Design is guided by the conviction that design is a powerful tool of communication and influence; a strategic asset that directly serves the objectives of its clients. Mauk Design believes that effective design rests upon an in-depth understanding of a client's business needs.

People go to trade shows and events to see the next big thing, or to see an existing product or service in a new way. Mauk Design focus on delivering in that difficult environment by showing products in special and unexpected ways. The firm creates jaw-dropping spectacles and experiences that can engage the visitor from a distance and then provide a sophisticated interaction once they are drawn in.

As one of the few firms that works predominantly on trade show design, Mauk works closely with its clients, asking difficult questions that get to the essence of the story. Then, an extensive process of visualization and education slowly connects the design vision with the strategic business focus.

Ultimately a show environment tells an impressive story on a small scale. Once the audience is drawn in, the space should envelop them with a dimensional narrative that is tactile, visual, and audible. The great exhibit is not just about connecting the visitor with the brand, but leaving them with a lasting image.

Adobe headquarters lobby
This 20 by 25 foot (6x7.6m)
"color swatch" palette is
taken from Adobe Illustrator's
software interface and was
designed to infuse Adobe's
identity and software into
the lobby of its corporate
headquarters. In the morning,
sunlight washes through
the color swatches, painting
color across the lobby as the
employees enter the building.
At night, lights reverse the
effect, serving as a colorful
icon to the street.

Volkswagen Beetle booth, Miami Auto Show

Visitors to this exhibit were encouraged to immerse their senses in the Volkswagen aesthetic. Mauk's interactive design involved audio, visual, and tactile elements. Much of the exhibit was made of recycled materials, such as skateboard wheels, mountain climbing rope, car mirrors, polished aluminum scaffolding, and even stainless steel dogs' water bowls. To emphasize Volkswagen's reputation for safety, car seat belts were used to secure flower vases to the walls. To show the range of colors available for the Beetle, Mauk painted bowling balls, which were then attached to a wall. As well as adding a striking visual element to the exhibit, this also made it more interactive as visitors were encouraged to spin the balls. This exhibit was honored with *EXHIBITOR Magazine*'s 20/20 award for the best visionary design of the next 20 years.

PlayStation exhibition, Los Angeles

In this 200 by 200 foot (60.9x60.9m) exhibition an illuminated helix of blue side-emitting fiber optics served as a visual icon for the revolutionary BluRay disc of the next generation of PlayStation. To demonstrate the PlayStation Portable (PSP), a pavilion with an illuminated floor and overhead cloud graphics created a serenity that contrasted with the loud, high-energy atmosphere of the rest of the show. Rows of spherical transparent hanging chairs became sound-blocking demo stations that enabled each attendee to have a personal experience with the PSP.

**Duncan Aviation,
traveling exhibition**
Duncan Aviation is a
business-jet maintenance
company and a long-standing
client of Mauk Design. Since
Duncan Aviation and all its
competitors utilize similar
facilities and equipment, this
exhibition used a canopy of
portraits of each of Duncan's
2,200 employees to make the
company stand out. An
illuminated jet flew across
the sky above the portraits.
The veneer desk speaks to
Duncan's skill in aircraft
interior cabinetry as it was
built in the company's own
shop. The aluminum fin
museum cases showcase
items from aircraft sales.

Pentagram

With offices in New York, San Francisco, Austin, London, and Berlin, Pentagram is a world leader in graphic, product, building, and environmental design, as well as exhibition design. Its modern sensibilities as well as its boldness has made it one of the most award-winning and recognizable design firms.

The firm's structure is built around equal design partners, each of whom have the responsibility of managing a project team. These teams can work independently or collaborate with other teams. Since each of the partners has their own skill sets and point of view, the resulting work is very diverse, but the culture of the firm permeates every project. Pentagram's work is characterized by the use of crisp materials, a restrained use of color and light, and simplicity and directness in information communication. The partners are spread around the world, giving their work a global outlook. Pentagram collaborates closely with clients on ongoing programs that can lead in multiple directions, including identity programs, wayfinding, or exhibitions.

The final success of Pentagram is its ability to keep its growing stable of star designers together in one firm. Partners such as Abbott Miller, Michael Bierut, and Paula Scher have attained international design star status. Their ability to retain their own distinct design identities while also collaborating under the banner of one firm, shows that Pentagram may be a model for the future.

United Airlines hangar mural, Logan International Airport, Boston
Pentagram was asked by its long-time client, United Airlines, to develop a graphic façade for a new hangar in Logan International Airport. The resulting mural shows interpretation at an enormous scale, with an x-ray taken of a passenger plane and applied to the wall of a hangar. The criteria for the design were that it needed to feel distinctly United and that it be a visual event with the potential to become an airport landmark for those flying into and out of Boston. Working with a photographer specializing in x-ray images, the concept for the 17,000 square foot (5,182m²) design depicts a full-scale x-ray image of

United's flagship aircraft, the Boeing 777, being serviced by United mechanics. The design was intended to underscore United's commitment to safety, and to recognize the individuals behind the scenes who make it possible. The image references the unique structure of the new building as well, by uncovering the form of actual architectural elements below the skin of the hangar. Stylistically, it draws upon the image of the security x-ray already familiar to any air traveler. This simple gesture provides multiple meanings to the millions of drivers who pass by the facility yearly, contrasting the fragility of the human pilots with the power of the machinery.

future
of the sea

café

The National Maritime Museum

Wayfinding and identity elements in a museum facility must be simple and direct. The National Maritime Museum displays large-scale objects inside a grand, detailed exhibition space. The identifying signs take on the appearance of sails delicately attached to the building that dynamically, but unobstrusively complement the objects.

***Harley-Davidson
100th Anniversary
Open Road Tour,*
traveling exhibition**
Honoring a legacy brand
which is also a cultural
icon demands careful
acknowledgment of the past
while also providing a vital
image of the present and
future. Starting from the
fundamental brand elements
of Harley-Davidson, such as
the colors black and orange,
the machines themselves,
and even the sound of the
engine rumble, this traveling
exhibition has a state fair
feeling about it, which
references the cult gathering
of bikers. The bikes are clearly
the hero in this design and all
the design elements are in
support of highlighting these
great machines.

The Gutenberg Bible display case, The Ransom Center

The Ransom Center at the University of Texas at Austin houses 30 million literary manuscripts, one million rare books, five million photographs, and over one hundred thousand works of art. Highlights include *The Gutenberg Bible* (c. 1455) and the world's first photograph (c. 1826). The cases for both these artifacts are displayed in the lobby of the Center and are viewed in such a way that best represents their individual histories, without obscuring the entrance. The displays allow the viewer to walk around and fully experience the objects. The strength of the materials in the exhibition is reminiscent of an era when solid, masculine materials

What Pat Moynihan Said About That, The Municipal Art Society of New York

This memorial exhibition for the legendary, outspoken New York Senator Daniel Patrick Moynihan was mounted by Moynihan's friends and colleagues as a personal tribute to his life through words and pictures. This show was designed as a temporary tribute space, and was inexpensively assembled using fabric and vinyl ink-jet banners and images. This exhibition packs a tremendous punch on a limited budget, a simple palette of materials, and in a small single room by effectively utilizing the grand interior architecture in this former Villard mansion, now the home of The Municipal Art Society of New York. The design carries forth the message very powerfully and elegantly by engaging the large curved window openings for Moynihan's quotes and turning the typewriter into a powerful landmark element.

Box & Cox

Since the 1980s, the South Korean economy has grown to become the seventh largest in the world. Alongside this rapid growth, the design community has developed its own character with firms like Box & Cox designing exciting and unique environments that take full advantage of rich Korean traditions in art, language, and technology. Drawing on a cultural history of layering space, typographical artistry, and creative icon development, Box & Cox has developed a unique approach to creating spaces that communicate on multiple levels.

A key Korean cultural tradition is geomancy, the use of divination to balance the forces of good and evil. This involves specific approaches toward the location of buildings, the layout of interiors, and the distance between objects, creating free-flowing spaces. Box & Cox has taken this tradition of spatial balance and used it to inspire its own work.

Box & Cox's work utilizes transparency, color, layer, and language to create spaces that can be defined as complete environments, as paths of circulation, or as collections of discreet objects to be viewed. Large-scale graphics are interwoven with glass, fabric, furniture, and walls to immerse audiences in comforting places that provide few demands on viewing or interpretation. The spaces are also carefully balanced to provide visitors with either a leisurely overview or an in-depth examination of the subject.

Canny Village, Pundang
Designed with Mileseum. This exhibition for children uses inexpensive layered digital printing to explain recycling processes. The characters of the Korean language are mixed with icons and other graphics to develop an internal exhibition language, which is simple for children to navigate and comprehend.

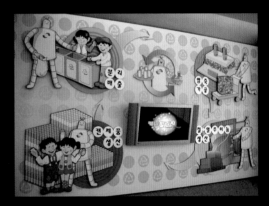

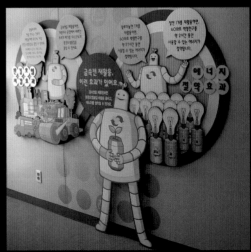

***DEX Design Experience*, Seoul**
Designed with GL Associates.
This exhibition of Korean
design history layers objects
with historical narratives. The
objects and stories are given
a great deal of room to be read
as discreet objects in space
instead of as a distinct path,
by floating them in transparent
boxes at different heights.

2004 Dong-A, LG International Festival of Comics and Animation, Seoul

In Korea, cartoons and comics are treated as sophisticated art forms. This exhibition combines many elements that are part of the Box & Cox philosophy, including graphics on multiple surfaces, utilizing light to accent distinct aspects of the show, and balancing design elements to create one cohesive space.

**Left: SeongJu Kayasan
Wildflower Botanical
Garden, Kayasan
National Park
Right: Samsung
Total Museum**
Botanical Garden designed
with Mileseum. These displays
show Box & Cox's extensive
use of unique materials to
create exhibition centerpieces
as well as paths and barriers.
The Botanical Garden uses
foliage integrated with wall
surfaces to define the
exhibition. The Samsung
museum uses glass to
envelop and structure
the space.

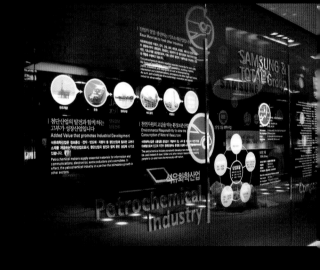

Casson Mann

In a lecture given by Dinah Casson in 1999 she described her firm thus: "We work out of central London and because most of London is nineteenth century or earlier, much of our work has been concerned with issues of inserting new into old. Since 1983 we have had a good time and not much money. Generally, we have had good clients, (always at the bottom of the successful projects), few bad debts, and we have spent too long on everything."

This is a perfect description of Casson Mann, a firm that, in spite of its extensive exhibition design work, still thinks of itself as an interior designer, molding space, materials, and light. Its approach to exhibition work is to fuse the objects and information being displayed with the interior space in a way that conveys the fundamental style behind the objects being presented. Casson Mann's work is highly tactile and interactive; it uses the term "collaboration" to define the personal interaction between the visitor and the objects on display. The firm accepts the primacy of the display object, but also allows for personal interaction.

Casson Mann is made up of designers and architects, and avoids traditional job hierarchies. This employment structure is reflected in its design approach; design elements are broken down into areas of equal importance to avoid structural hierarchies. This has allowed the firm to try its hand in all areas of exhibition design, interiors, branded environments, and even product design.

Sparking Reaction,
Sellafield Visitor Centre
Sparking Reaction is an educational exhibition, highlighting the pros and cons of nuclear energy. Casson Mann's approach to this design was to help visitors engage with written text in an issues-based exhibition—something most people often do little of in this situation. The physically and intellectually immersive space at the center of _Sparking Reaction_ aims to do this with large-scale animated text and images projected onto the floor and walls. The text is revealed and concealed in a series of animations that intrigue and draw in visitors, and is updated with visitors' opinions. Steel polyhedral forms painted in pink UV-reactive paint house interactives, and a pink UV-lit tunnel leads to the entirely red Immersion Cinema—the first interactive cinema in the UK.

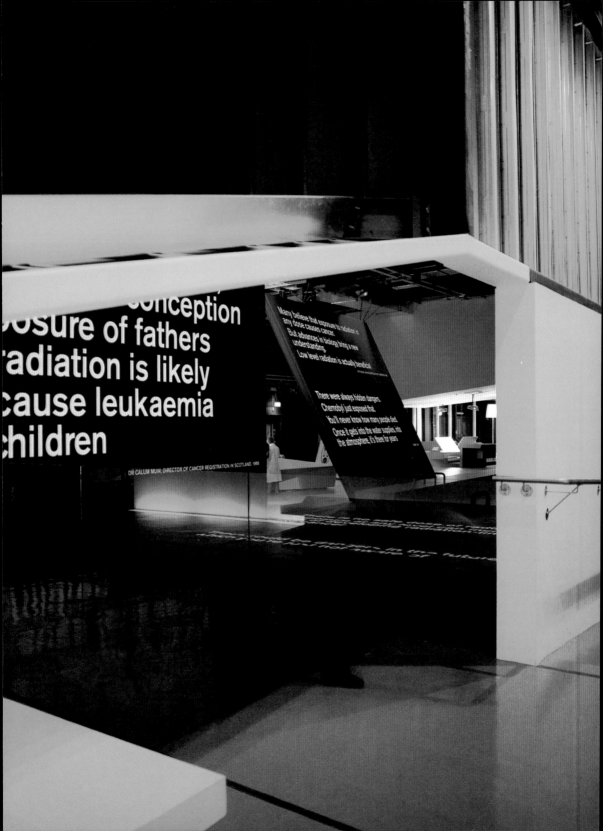

**Crimes Against Humanity,
Imperial War Museum**
The centerpiece of this
exhibition is a specially
commissioned 30 minute film,
which examines the theme of
genocide and ethnic conflict.
There is also a small
interactive area in the gallery
for those interested in deeper
research. The film, shocking
and harrowing in parts,
required a design approach
that spoke softly and trod
carefully, creating a space
that seemed neutral and
without distraction. Any
choice the visitor makes
about where and how to
watch the film or carry out
research on the databases
(alone, in a group, from the
sidelines) is deliberately
public, and open to
observation. Casson Mann
felt that it was important to
move the auditorium space
away from associations with
the comfort and anonymity
of the theater.

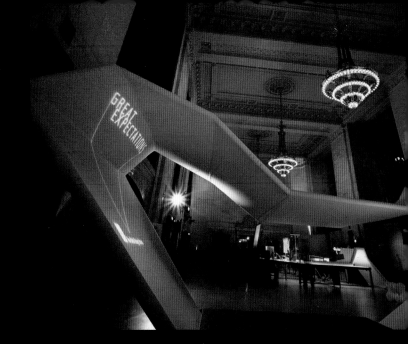

Great Expectations, Grand Central Station

This exhibition formed part of the UKwithNY festival, which aims to raise the profile of British products and services in New York. The venue was Grand Central Station; a place people usually just hurry through. Casson Mann wanted to stop visitors in their tracks, so the design had to be dramatic, playful, and easily accessible. The exhibition is built around an illuminated 164 foot (50m) long banquet table, covered in design products. The intention was to suggest and encourage conversation and dialogue. Speakers in the chairs and monitors set into the table offered visitors explanations of the objects on display.

Who am I?,
The Science Museum

The purpose of this exhibition is to examine how modern science is transforming our understanding of what it means to be human. Casson Mann wanted the design for *Who am I?* to reflect the excitement of innovation, and propel visitors toward self-discovery. Just as the galleries are about the future of science rather than its history, the main concept for the design was about ideas, not about objects. The firm created landscapes that underpinned the themes and galleries that themselves became part of the story.

Did we all come from Z...

By passing on their
ancestors partly de
are. By studying and
can now investigate
humans migrated a
But genetics can't t
archaeology and li
important, too.

To find out more, se

African origins

Ralph Appelbaum Associates

Ralph Appelbaum Associates (RAA) is a group of planners, designers, and producers of museum exhibitions, visitor centers, and educational environments with subject areas ranging from natural history and the physical sciences, to cultural, social, and corporate history, sports, and the fine arts. Currently the largest interpretive museum design firm in the world, RAA has an interdisciplinary staff of more than 75 specialists based in New York, Beijing, and London.

RAA is best known for large-scale, permanent museum projects requiring a marriage of complex educational content with physical environments, but the firm specializes in addressing the fundraising, management, and operational needs that allow museums to function. This is evident in its largest projects in which the smooth functioning of the museum staff and the ongoing maintenance is every bit as crucial as the physical structure of the exhibition.

Beginning with its work for the United States Holocaust Memorial Museum, RAA has developed a signature and pioneering approach of using objects and interpretive elements, not just as pieces to be interpreted, but as elements in the creation of powerful reflective spaces. Working with leading architects, including Pei Cobb Freed, the spaces RAA creates leave visitors with lingering memories of the central ideas behind a museum. With the addition of multimedia technologies, such as multiple LED screens, the spaces also become powerful stages for educational content.

***We the People*, National Constitution Center**
This exhibition is housed inside a facility that is also used for traveling shows and ongoing scholarship. Using both high-tech multimedia projection screens and "low-tech" sculptures, post-it notes, and human guides, the exhibition both teaches the history of the US Constitution and forces the audience to be a participant in the ideas behind the document. The exhibition concludes with a room containing life-size sculptures of the signers of the Constitution, bringing immediacy to the idea of a special document created at a particular place and time.

7

National Museum of Prehistory

This is the first museum to incorporate the important archaeological research and the results of excavations in Taiwan, and present a comprehensive story of the island's prehistoric cultures. The installation has a fine blend of high-quality displays and interpretations of archaeological objects and information within a rich, contemporary exhibition environment. Centered around a landmark glass keystone structure, the vibrant, deep color palette and rich wood enliven the concept of archaeology and give it an immediacy and directness. The use of contemporary video and computer interactives are thoughtfully integrated into the environment, very effectively coexisting with tableaux and object displays.

Corning Museum of Glass

This project challenged RAA to bring the diverse elements of a large corporate entity into focus by unifying stories of the science and industry of glassmaking with the museum's ongoing traditions of glass collecting and community involvement. The enormous complexity of information presented runs the danger of confusing the visitor, but a skillful balancing of interactive exhibitions and objects provides a clear, if dense, structure. The museum is designed as a series of pavilions. These pavilions in turn center around glass artwork or science exhibitions that each contain a signature landmark element.

National Holocaust Museum

This historic and trendsetting museum is often called "the first twenty-first century museum." Beginning with a modern structure designed by architecture firm Pei Cobb Freed, the museum contains incredibly powerful spaces that display artifacts from Holocaust victims and survivors. The museum treats the objects with reverence, extending beyond interpretation, into evoking an emotional response from the audience. The display shown here is made up of thousands of archived photographs, which were integrated into one powerful, introspective gallery

Steuben flagship store
This store design transmits the culture of Steuben through its appearance and educational videos, making it more accessible and creating a framework for continuing change. The designers changed the relationship between the object and the customer, inviting people to congregate around the circular display tables and experience the glass intimately, thus creating a museum-like educational experience in a retail environment.

Reich + Petch

Reich + Petch is a multidisciplinary firm of architects and designers working in exhibition, interior, industrial, and environmental design. Based in Toronto, Reich + Petch is inspired by opportunities to create imaginative, interactive spaces that are meaningful and engaging for the end user. This drive to explore, innovate, and shape environments that excite the senses and make an emotional connection with visitors is the central theme of the firm's work. Director Tony Reich describes its work as "experience architecture and design." This approach results in environments that are focused around objects and stories, but do not force the audience forward, allowing them to explore at their own pace instead. Exhibitions also focus on using material, space, lighting and texture to create subtle mood shifts between objects and displays.

Reich + Petch works in collaboration with clients and their stakeholders and has developed techniques to win consensus for design solutions through an interactive process. This involves exploring the audience experience with the client and defining what that may mean in built form. Further process refinement includes information programming, which in turn is enveloped by space and environmental controls to enhance the visitor experience. This process helps in creative decision-making and implementation as it demystifies the design approach and achieves an early buy-in. The design workshops are upbeat and exciting and the results are often surprising and innovative. The firm dovetails this work with other disciplines so that there is a common language of design and implementation, critical to architectural and digital means of communication.

The firm has developed large-scale casinos and resorts, as well as museums, visitor centers, and art galleries. This focus on large-scale thematic design with an international perspective—it has developed projects in 22 countries—requires large collaborative teams. Resulting exhibitions often have a close relationship with the natural and built environment, with a comfortable flow between exhibitions and the surrounding space.

Bug House gallery, World Museum Liverpool
The Bug House gallery takes visitors into the world of insects by arranging the exhibits around the theme of a house. Gallery rooms include the "nursery," "lounge," "study," and "garden." In the "kitchen" live specimens, static exhibits, and hands-on games illustrate aspects of feeding and food sources. Interactive games and animatronics throughout provide the element of memorable learning by fun and surprise. Exaggerated scale and perspective make the experience less scary for young children.

Right and below: World Cultures galleries, World Museum Liverpool
In these galleries materials, lighting, and textures are used to immerse the visitor in the change of mood between artifact displays relating to different geographic areas around the world. Floor, ceiling, and wall details provide a sense of enclosure for the artifacts that matches the cultural themes being exhibited.

Above and top: The Sir Christopher Ondaatje South Asian gallery, Royal Ontario Museum
The entrance to this gallery uses a pulsed multimedia show comprising 75 suspended mini TV monitors to represent a metaphor of a village tree in the Indian subcontinent. The feature is in turn used as an audio-visual storytelling device. An "object theater" approach is used to provide a means of storytelling by members of the community who relate their impressions of the artifacts displayed.

The Saudi Arabian National Museum

The Saudi Arabian National Museum presents the natural, cultural, and ethnographic history of the Kingdom in nine multimedia galleries. Reconstructions of vernacular architecture from the different regions and provinces set the context for the display of ethnographic artifacts. The exhibits and architecture are integrated to reinforce the storyline through the circulation in a gallery devoted to the Hajj and the holy sites of Mecca and Medina. Reich + Petch used sculptural abstract forms like curves and screens to envelop the reconstructions without dominating them.

Kenneth E. Behring Hall of Mammals, Smithsonian Institution National Museum of Natural History
This gallery combines specimens, interactive multimedia, dramatic theatrics, and hands-on interactives. The animals are arranged in sets of poses, to teach the audience about their daily activities.

Step into a Cold, Cold World

Discover how northern mammals stay warm and
find food in one of the harshest environments on Earth.

How do polar bears
stay warm all winter?

The Lake Superior Provincial Park Visitor Centre

The building, interiors, exhibits, and graphics were all designed under one process. The building exterior is used to display interpretive environmental graphics in the direct context of Lake Superior. The casts of fish are viewed with the horizon of the lake water line as the background, as exterior graphic panels interpret the stories about them. Because all the design elements were created at one time, the inside and outside of the buildings are expressed as one element with long distance vistas combining with detailed captions and displays.

C&G Partners

The New York-based firm C&G Partners is dedicated to multidisciplinary communication design projects. Whether creating exhibitions, environments, identities, print, signage, or interactive experiences, the method is always the same: start with a deep immersion into what makes each project special. The firm sets out to make experiences memorable, not to impose a preset style. Strong, unifying ideas can produce work that is meaningful, relevant, and always current.

The firm's idea-based approach often results in projects that have a strong physical or conceptual center that can drive stories and make memories for the audience. These central design features can be major sculptural elements, powerful spaces, or simply clear pathways. All the interpretive and interactive elements of the exhibitions are designed to support this central idea.

C&G Partners was founded by Steff Geissbuhler, Keith Helmetag, Jonathan Alger, and Emanuela Frigerio. Previously, the partners were principals at the well-known design firm Chermayeff & Geismar Inc., from which C&G takes its name. The partners' cumulative history includes the creation of some of the world's most recognizable experiences, images, spaces, and icons.

US Patent and Trademark Office Museum

This highly flexible exhibition system allows video monitors, artifact displays, and rear-illuminated photographs to be arranged at will. Each module contains a state-of-the-art LED strip to accommodate changing display captions, along with a complex switching system that synchronizes lighting, sound effects, and pneumatic motion components. This innovative system was awarded its own patent from the Office.

The Griffith Observatory

The Griffith Observatory is one of the most visited public observatories in the world. Recently renovated and updated, it now hosts 20,000 square feet (6,096m²) of new exhibits about the one thing that all humans have always had in common: the sky. Projects include "The Big Picture," a tilting, 150 x 20 foot (45.75 x 6m) porcelain enamel panoramic image of the universe that is the largest astronomical image ever produced. Some of these exhibitions include detailed lit models and large-scale projected images of galactic phenomenon. The lighting is dark to give the audience an intimate experience with the displays.

The Good Housekeeping Research Institute has been educating and protecting American women and their families since 1900.

Good Housekeeping Promises

JOY IN A BOTTLE BEATS

Above: Good Housekeeping Institute

The Good Housekeeping Institute is the consumer product evaluation laboratory of *Good Housekeeping* magazine. This exhibition was designed to celebrate the Institute's commitment to consumers' and women's advocacy. Interactive stations display the history of the famous magazine and its Good Buys awards program. The exhibits are adjacent to the Institute's test kitchen and appliance laboratories, giving visitors a true behind-the-scenes experience. Originally

Opposite: The Jefferson Library, Library of Congress

When the original Library of Congress was burned in the War of 1812, Thomas Jefferson sold his personal library of about 6,500 books to the government to replace it. To commemorate the library's bicentennial, a special exhibition on Jefferson was developed. The exhibition helps to illuminate the intellectual background of one of the most revered figures in American history. Designed at Chermayeff & Geismar Inc. by Jonathan Alger in collaboration

1988 SEOUL

1992 BARCELONA

Above: *Faster, Higher, Stonger*, Time Warner Center
This exhibition celebrates *Sports Illustrated* magazine's rich history of Olympic photography. The exhibition architecture makes bold use of the traditional Olympic symbol of interconnected rings, seeming to cut through the structure of the building itself, implying speed, grace, and sport.

Left: The Money Museum, The Federal Reserve Bank of Atlanta
The Money Museum was created to give visitors a firsthand experience of what happens behind the facade of the bank. The canted, curving display tells the history of the world through the history of money, from the days of barter economies to e-commerce. Perimeter alcoves use case studies, animated maps, and film to explain the complex procedures of the bank. Visitors can touch a glass case containing millions or they can take a virtual journey inside the bank's vast underground vault.

Below: The John Heinz National Wildlife Refuge at Tinicum Marsh
The centerpiece of the exhibits at The John Heinz National Wildlife Refuge at Tinicum Marsh is a detailed, diorama cross section designed to reveal the secrets of the marsh and impart the value of wetlands. The diorama serves as both the form and the path that drives the story. This project won an American Institute of Architects Committee on the Environment award.

The objective of Melbourne-based emerystudio is to discover the essence of something, explain why it is plain and ordinary the way it is, then transform it by placing it into a new realm that's inexplicable and extraordinary. The aim is to reveal the essence of that thing, give it expression and meaning, and trigger emotional connections and responses that will provoke the desired response from the audience. It's about throwing the viewers' certainties out of balance, challenging preconceptions and established conventions.

Today the firm is engaged in a diversity of projects and design disciplines, working across two, three, and four-dimensional spatial environments in brand identity, print, multimedia, exhibitions, and environmental graphic design. In a way, emerystudio has become a "specialist generalist" encompassing a broad scope of design activities, including designing for the written word and for the moving image, designing exhibitions, the ordering and identity of urban spaces from the scale of single buildings to whole cities, and designing for corporate communications and branding. But whatever the task or the medium, the focus is around complete design control.

emerystudio's roots are in traditional graphic design and typography. Through a long-standing interest in architecture, urban design, and art, however, the firm has established for itself a central position for design work in the built environment.

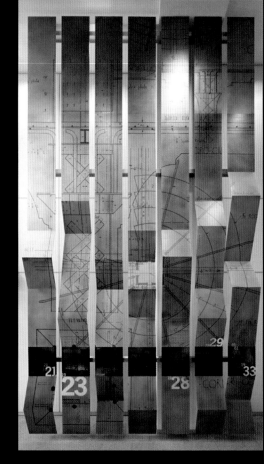

Herald and Weekly Times building, Melbourne
The Herald and Weekly Times building is of heritage significance. When the site was redeveloped into an office tower much of the original building fabric was retained. However, the printing industry heritage features were lost. These features have been recreated through a series of installations narrating the building's former use. Etched metal panels refer to the printing plates used in the printing process from a past era. Large metal panels, articulated as ribbons cascading from the ceiling, reflect the forms of the newspapers flowing through the presses.

Australian Racing Museum

The Australian Racing Museum combines sporting, social, and natural history themes. An important objective is to bring the world of horse racing to the attention of a new, young generation. The exhibition design and its architectural spaces are the outcome of close collaboration between emerystudio and Spowers architects. An important feature of the museum is the way that conventional distinctions between exhibition design and architecture are blurred. The exhibits on display include the skeleton of Carbine, winner of the 1890 Melbourne Cup and one of Australia's greatest horses. The skeleton has been brought to life via a liquid crystal screen placed next to it on which an animated sequence is projected. The virtual horse has been digitally "built" and several stories are told, including animations explaining the operation of the horse's heart, lungs, and legs. Through the drama of multimedia, lighting, soundscape, digital visual effects, and their integration with the exhibition spaces, new life is breathed into the objects, artifacts, and personalities of racing's history. In other areas of the exhibition, glass display cases are combined with wall surfaces and graphics to create an immersive experience that merges display and interior.

Right: *lab.3000 Digital Design Biennale*, Melbourne Museum
Designed by Tom Kovac with graphics by emerystudio. "Imagining the Future" was the theme for the inaugural *lab.3000 Digital Design Biennale*, an international exhibition that showcases digital art and the ways in which it impacts on every facet of our daily lives. "Imagining the Future" supposed a multidisciplinary platform where innovation is driven by sustainability, where science meets art, and the future of design is now. emerystudio's contribution to the project was to design an overhead display comprising 459 feet (140m) of text and images, communicating current international innovators and mentors in digital design. The sinuous 229 foot (70m) long display element is in the form of an infinity symbol, taking design cues from the lab.3000 brand identity. emerystudio was also responsible for the design of the exhibition catalog, the lab.3000 branding, and various digitally animated and printed marketing communications materials.

Right and opposite: PMP Limited office, Melbourne
The architect Bates Smart and PMP, a media production and magazine distribution company, requested a three-dimensional, textural, dramatically up-lit installation located in a double-height office reception space. An abstract work that refers to the activities of the business, the object is designed to create a spatial focus and to be a feature. The scheme refers to streams of digital information and the notion of a performance indicator.

development of content-generated spaces in its designs for museums, trade fairs, and large events. As a general contractor, the company plans, designs, and constructs the architecture, graphics, lighting, and media of exhibitions.

Founded in 1997 in Stuttgart as a "laboratory of design," the firm quickly developed as a center of experimentation and is well established in the European exhibition design sector. atelierbrückner's aim is to generate space out of content, producing installations that arise from theatrical concepts, leading the visitor to the center of a specific story. The firm's mantra is "form follows content," putting placemaking at the center of the storytelling process.

atelierbrückner seeks to develop the relationships between architecture and exhibition design, between an exhibition and its content, and between content and the audience. The term atelierbrückner uses for this design approach is "Gesamtkunstwerk," meaning the creation of an entire work of art by using harmonious relationships between form and content and experimenting with space, graphics, light, and media.

This approach stems from the multidisciplinary makeup of the firm. Its staff members have experience in architecture, stage design, interior design, light design, communication and graphic design, product design, and art history. For each project, a team is set up of employees who complement one another in education and experience. The resulting work crosses over from exhibition to pavilion to public space to public art.

Blue Gardens, trade show booth for Panasonic, IFA 2001

The aim of this booth was to bring together all of Panasonic's heterogeneous product lines in one integrative design. A 985 foot (300m) long and 13 foot (4m) tall Möbius strip was covered with film, projected by 52 high-end video beamers, impressively demonstrating the competence and capability of Panasonic products. Visitors became immersed in a world of moving images.

Cyclebowl pavilion for the Duales System AG, Expo 2000

This pavilion design is a multidisciplinary synthesis of architecture, scenography, graphics, sound, light, film, and even an artificial tornado created by a wind machine. The past, present, and future of recycling management were shown in three themed areas on an exhibition path of three mounting ramps. This was one of the few pavilions at Expo 2000 which functioned both as a daylight exhibition building and as a black box for shows that needed controlled lighting.

German Sports and Olympic Museum

This museum takes visitors on a journey through 200 years of German sports history. Speed and movement come together in this exhibition design, where the illusion of movement is coupled with exciting juxtapositions of forms to create layered flowing environments.

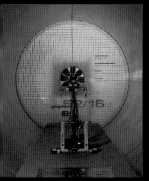

Right: Research laboratory, Westphalian State Museum of Archaeology

At the researcher's laboratory the archaeological investigation of findings is staged as a criminal case. Fourteen containers with specific pieces of information for solving a crime are laid out as interactive exhibits which take the form of the working atmosphere of a CSI lab. By recreating the experience of sitting at a work table, information can be displayed intimately.

Above, left, and far left:
***Expedition Titanic*,**
Hamburg docklands
As one of the most successful thematic exhibitions of recent years, *Expedition Titanic* claims pioneer status among popular scientific exhibitions. The aim was to approach the story of the *Titanic* using subtly designed theme rooms. To allow visitors to interpret the spaces, an associative rather than a didactic concept was chosen, with the rooms arranged as a sequence of themes and atmospheres to be read like a book. The intention was to build up emotions in the visitor, so they would feel deeply affected by the fate of the *Titanic* and its passengers.

GL Associates

Exhibition designers strive to create environments that are not just interesting to navigate, but also are enjoyable and comfortable places to be. GL Associates is a design firm based in Seoul that is focused on creating exhibitions that engage the audience through tactile sophistication and subtle enclosure of space.

GL Associates' work merges commercial interior design with exhibition design. The resulting collaboration between these two groups exhibitions with the quality of a piece of furniture or sculpture. Exhibitions are focused at the human level with seating, desks, and tables merged into the displays to provide a level of comfort for the audience. Many of the firm's exhibitions also have subtle enclosures built into them in some way to draw the audience into comfortable spaces. This is particularly evident in the firm's trade show and corporate displays, which create small oases of calm space in the cacophony of the convention environment.

The firm is a pioneer in branded environments in Korea, partnering with international branding agencies, such as Lippincott Mercer, to create exhibitions that match the design aesthetic and quality of a company's offices, marketing materials, and retail displays, while providing information at a high level. These international partnerships have also spread to institutions and schools, combining GL Associates' design approach with content developers from around the world.

The Ultra Edition 8.4
SGH-Z370

LIMITS
GSM/GPRS/EDGE (900/1800/1900MHz)
2 Megapixel Camera & VGA Camera for Video Telephony
Display : 262144 Color TFT (1.9",220x176)
External Memory: microSD
Multi-format music/video player with Digital Power Amp
Bluetooth stereo Music Profile (A2DP)
Document viewer
Offline Mode
vSearch and Black GUI
113x49x6.4mm

**Samsung Ultra Edition 3G
cellphone exhibition,
the Louvre Museum**
This corporate exhibition
inside the Louvre aimed to
show off Samsung's Ultra
Edition range of cellphones,
which were designed to be
the world's thinnest 3G
phones. GL Associates had a
number of technical barriers
to surmount, the most
important of which was to
unobtrusively fit the exhibit
inside the museum's busy
entrance areas. The exhibition
slopes at a gentle angle over
the audience, creating subtle
enclosures and gateways to
engage the visitor.

Hold an *Anycall*, and you're
holding the whole world.

Samsung Anycall
Studio, Seoul

This corporate exhibition for
Samsung utilizes bright colors
and round shapes to create
an informal lounge where
visitors can interact with the
company's latest offerings
while sitting in comfortable
chairs, seated at desks, or
standing at kiosks. The goal
is to provide an environment
that people want to return
to again and again to try out
new products.

CARING
ARTISTIC
FIRM
HELPING
GIFTED

Samsung Digital Media Gallery, 2005 Korea Electronics Show

This exhibition designed for Samsung uses pods of space, either as furniture, fixtures, or signs, to create displays inside of displays. GL Associates' goal was to create successive enclosures that drew the audience into ever more refined presentations. The use of technology also becomes greater farther into the exhibition to engage the more prepared audience.

**She's Like a Rainbow/
Color and Fashion**,
**Samsung Art and Design
Institute and the Fashion
Institute of Technology**

The space in this exhibition is
kept open and uncluttered so
that the visitor can see all the
objects at once before
focusing on specific
platforms. The explanatory
text panels are placed at
ground level, forcing the
visitor to see the objects first,
before reading about them in
more detail.

Hewitt Pender Associates

Hewitt Pender Associates' work is based on achieving longevity; the Sydney-based firm aims to produce monuments, visitor centers, and museums that will remain relevant for 10 to 20 years; a life span that is an eternity for exhibitions. To ensure that exhibitions stay relevant, the firm has developed a rigorous 10-part design program. This includes avoiding fashionable graphic communication styles that can date quickly, avoiding the use of unnecessary technology, and providing a worthwhile reward to visitors to encourage word-of-mouth recommendation.

The firm's experience is that the most successful projects in the long run are those with credibility and uniqueness. Uniqueness can be built in with special presentations or technologies, but credibility can only be gained by location and a direct connection to the subject. Credibility is often achieved in Hewitt Pender's work through a careful balance of historical context with modern convenience, a careful touch on the landscape, and a reverence for the subject.

Museum of Wellington City and Sea

Built in 1892 as a bonded warehouse and later used as Harbour Board offices, the Bond Store in Wellington, New Zealand is now the home of the Museum of Wellington City and Sea. Hewitt Pender's design carefully combines the original architectural features of the Bond Store with the requirements of modern museums. All additions made to the building's interior since 1900 were removed, and a section of each of the three floors was cut away to reveal more of the original structure and to make way for a central staircase to improve access for visitors. Traditional displays of artifacts are offset by interactive exhibits, holographs, and a giant cinema screen that takes up an entire wall.

The Antarctic Attraction, International Antarctic Centre

The International Antarctic Centre in Christchurch, New Zealand, was established to support scientific programs and is home to the New Zealand, US, and Italian Antarctic programs. Hewitt Pender was commissioned to design a visitor center within the existing Antarctic Centre. The visitor center uses immersive and interactive exhibitions to recreate the atmosphere and environment of Antarctica. For the "Snow and Ice Experience," the designers created a 656 square foot (200m^2) refrigerated zone that uses real snow and ice and a wind chill machine to immerse the audience in the conditions of the Antarctic. For less adventurous visitors, there is a viewing lounge that allows them to be included in the experience.

Hellfire Pass Memorial Museum

The Hellfire Pass Memorial Museum in Thailand commemorates those who worked and died during the building of the Burma–Thailand Railway while they were prisoners of war of the Japanese in WWII. The museum's main gallery features a model of a cleared section of the railway and tells the story of its construction from when the first POWs arrived. Visitors can use monoculars to zoom in on various parts of the model. Weathered timber and rusted metal were used in the main exhibition support structure to refer to the original trestle bridges. A shaded and raised walkway offers visitors a space for peaceful contemplation (see central image). Museum visitors are encouraged to follow the 2½ mile (4km) walking trail, which follows the path of the original railroad (see image on right).

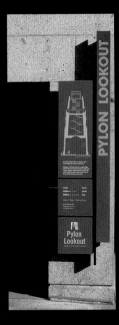

Pylon Lookout Museum, Sydney Harbour Bridge

Still the world's largest and heaviest steel bridge, this iconic Sydney landmark was opened in 1932 during the Great Depression years and, in terms of engineering prowess, put Australia on the world stage. Located in the bridge's southeastern pylon, the Pylon Lookout Museum contains three levels of exhibits revealing the history of the bridge. The "Dangerous Works" exhibits show how the bridge was built and highlight the dangers of the working conditions. The exhibit was modeled on photographs taken during construction. The design was severely restricted by the lack of access inside this heritage structure, so Hewitt Pender had to ensure that all space was used as effectively as possible.

Gold and Civilisation, traveling exhibition

This project was the curtain raiser for the new National Museum of Australia in Canberra, and contained priceless gold exhibits sent from all over the world. *Gold and Civilisation* explored the perceived value of gold, the effect it has on world societies, and how Australia has contributed to that phenomenon. This was an unusually high security exhibition indemnified by the Australian Government for an extremely high but undisclosed amount.

After appearing at the National Museum, the exhibition moved to the Melbourne Museum. The two gallery spaces were very different in shape, so the exhibition structure was designed to fit a long site and a square site, with the layout influenced by the position of floor service grids. Two major vertical elements were added to the exhibition structure to effectively use the volume of the gallery spaces. A large part of the project budget was spent on alarm systems to safeguard the priceless exhibits.

nendo

"Giving people a small '!' moment. There are so many small '!' moments hidden in our everyday lives. But we don't recognize them, and even when we do recognize them, we tend to unconsciously reset our minds and forget what we've seen. But we believe these small '!' moments are what make our days so interesting, so rich. That's why we want to reconstitute the everyday by collecting and reshaping it into something that's easy to understand. We'd like the people who've encountered nendo's designs to feel these small '!' moments intuitively. That's nendo's job."

This is the description that nendo, a multidisciplinary design firm based in Tokyo and Milan, gives for its approach to exhibitions, furniture, event spaces, and architecture. nendo strives to create exhibitions that resonate powerfully as spaces, objects, and themes, and to create small moments of clarity and delight for the audience.

nendo uses three devices: scale, materiality, and design integration to achieve this goal. Exhibition spaces are stretched or compressed, turned into jewel boxes or sprawling layers. Unique tactile materials, like wrapping paper or bubble wrap, are accentuated with sound and light to engage all the senses in the details of the exhibition. All the elements in nendo's exhibition designs are completely integrated, from the architecture and interior design to the graphics. This sense of cohesion gives each project a simple power and consistency.

nendo's work represents the adventurous spirit of the younger generation of designers pursuing exhibition design today. The future will doubtless see much greater integration of design disciplines, with firms like nendo leading the way.

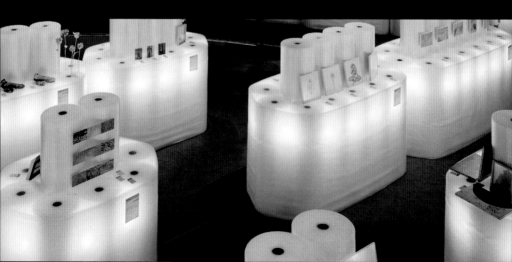

take art collection art fair, Spiral Garden
All of the products on sale at this "art department store" in Tokyo were limited editions, available only for the duration of the sale, but the sale also feels like an outlet store whose reasonably priced items are perfect as casual gifts. nendo wanted to bring out this unusual combination in the graphics and exhibition space, so they used materials like bubble wrap and craft wrap to create a mood like a department store's outlet. Exhibition stands made out of layered bubble wrap with embedded light sources highlighted each product, but when the event was over, they could be disassembled into sheets of bubble wrap and used as packing materials so that the exhibition didn't produce any waste. The firm printed posters, direct mail, invitations, envelopes, and special price tags in the shape of luggage tags on craft wrapping paper. Specific pictograms for each genre of product were based on luggage handling symbols to suggest the different sections in a department store.

NAOSHIMA STANDARD 2

This exhibition design counteracts a moody, ground-based rock garden memorial with a floating platform, using the difference between the heaviness of the exhibition and the lightness of the enclosure to dramatic effect.

Alice's Tea Party, **Living Design Center OZONE**
This event was held at Living Design Center OZONE in the Shinjuku district of Tokyo, to celebrate the 100th anniversary of English tea brand Lipton's presence in Japan. nendo designed a cafe based on the Mad Hatter's tea party in *Alice's Adventures in Wonderland*, radically distorting the size of the long table and rows of chairs to heighten the room's sense of receding depth.

Silhouettes of characters from the story were used as the pattern for the wallpaper, and were also distorted. These details create a space that feels long and narrow, as though it is pulling in visitors.

Trade show booth for BALS, 100% Design Tokyo

The BALS corporation owns a number of interiors brands, including Francfranc, J-PERIOD, BALS TOKYO, and AGITO, each inspired by a particular scene and lifestyle. nendo used the theme of roots as a motif for this booth to display products from all the BALS brands. Like roots, each of the brands is connected, but each one grows and expands in a different direction. New products that will appear on the shelves in the spring are gathering strength in the ground before they flower.

AMA-YADO LOUNGE

nendo believes that encountering a work of art at an exhibition can be similar to the chance meetings, random communication, and new opportunities that arise when you take shelter from a sudden downpour. This exhibition space used light and sound to create a scene of buckets being used to catch water falling from a leaky roof. *AMA-YADO LOUNGE* displayed furniture that nendo debuted at the Milano Salone and the Stockholm International Fair, along with new products.

Staples & Charles

Staples & Charles specializes in the craft of museum exhibition design, treating the collection and display of artifacts and information as a design language to be spoken with simplicity and clarity. The firm focuses on creating exhibitions around complex subjects in the arts, history, and humanities that require thoughtful and extensively researched solutions.

Staples & Charles often acts as both curator and designer on its projects, and can contribute to both the conception of exhibition ideas and the structure of storyline, so that text, artifacts, and design work together as a harmonious whole. The firm obsessively focuses on quality of fabrication and its relationship with fabricators, meticulously documenting even the smallest details of exhibitions. This combination of research and design disciplines still exists inside of large museums, and the firm carries that level of respect between historian, curator, interpreter, and designer.

This attention to research and detail pays off in exhibitions that do not initially wow the audience with spectacle, but draw the audience into the story and impress with the level of depth and detail. Staples & Charles' work is often housed inside famous sites or historic buildings, integrating the essence of the building form and plan into the exhibition.

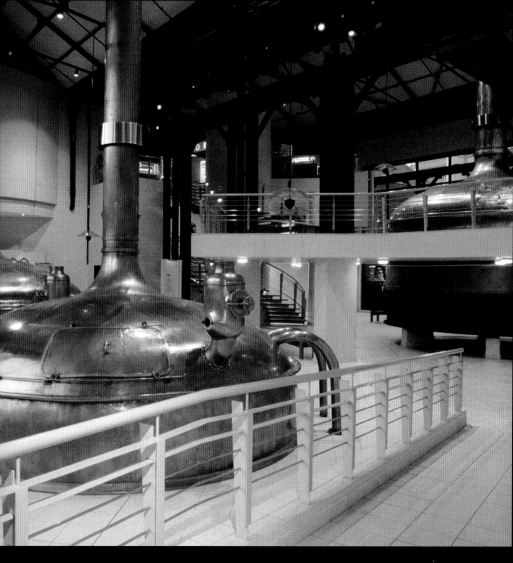

South African Breweries Centenary Centre

To celebrate its 100th anniversary, South African Breweries (SAB) built a 38,000 square foot (11,580m²) public pavilion to reflect the company's motto: "making beer, making friends." Theatrical settings with audio elements and an electro-mechanical puppet show help visitors trace the history of brewing from ancient times to the arrival of European brewing traditions in Africa and the formation of SAB in 1895. A specially created greenhouse introduces the ingredients that go into quality beer, while videos within historic brewing kettles explain the process of making it.

Class of 1956 Memorial Walkway, United States Military Academy at West Point

This is a permanent exhibition within a walkway between two sports facilities. The north wall charts the people, places, and events of the Cold War and the significant role played by graduates of West Point through texts, images, and globes. The south wall features large panels etched with quotes about "Duty, Honor, Country, and Character" to speak in more abstract terms of perseverance in difficult times. In the center is a memorial to class members who died in Vietnam. All of the materials—etched stainless steel, stone, images imbedded in glass, and bronze castings—were chosen for their durability. The quality of the materials and the simplicity of the display, combined with the functional elegance of the walkway structure, create a reverential experience.

The Sixth Floor Museum

The sixth floor of the former Texas School Book Depository, now the Dallas County Administrative Building, has been preserved and transformed into an exhibition that examines the death of President John F. Kennedy within the context of American cultural history. Staples & Charles worked closely with the restoration architect to preserve the mood and fabric of the old warehouse building to develop an appropriate space for a public exhibition. Staples & Charles also worked closely with the project director to develop the content and themes of the exhibition. At the end of the exhibition, visitors are asked to write comments in memory books.

Kahn Building, Yale University Art Gallery

When the New Art Gallery opened at Yale in 1953, the spacious and functional interior designed to provide a maximum of space, light, and flexibility was highly praised. Yet, within a few years, these very qualities were compromised by installations that sealed off the window walls and created smaller galleries within the open spaces. Now, the architectural fabric of Louis Kahn's first museum has been restored. Simultaneously, an overall approach to the installation of the permanent collection was developed that respects the building and the art, while meeting today's requirements for conservation and accessibility. Staples & Charles redesigned Kahn's legendary "pogo panels" that serve as moveable walls within the open galleries, and created a system of related platforms, pedestals, and cases.

World of Coca Cola

This corporate museum successfully mingles innovation and entertainment with memorabilia and nostalgia. Throughout the three-story pavilion, the company's extensive collection of advertising is displayed. A kinetic sculpture, the "Bottling Fantasy," welcomes visitors into the exhibition areas. Interactive videos in large Coke cans are sprinkled throughout. There are also two sit-down theaters, an historic soda fountain and a contemporary one where visitors can sample the products of the Coca-Cola company. Staples & Charles developed content with the company's archivist, designed the exhibitions, and worked closely with the architects on the flow and style of the public areas.

References

Books and articles

Architects and Exhibition Design. Eleanor Gawne. RIBA Heinz Gallery, 1998.

Acts of Meaning. Jerome Bruner. Harvard University Press, 1992.

Brandscaping: Worlds of Experience in Retail Design. Otto Riewoldt. Birkhauser, 2002.

Carlo Scarpa. Sergio Los. Taschen, 1994.

Contemporary Exhibit Design. Martin Pegler. HarperCollins Design, 2002.

Designing Exhibitions / Ausstellungen Entwerfen. Aurelia Bertron, Ulrich Schwarz, and Claudia Frey. Birkhauser, 2006.

Designing the World's Best Exhibits. Martin Pegler. Visual Reference Publications, 2003.

Eames Design. John Neuhart and Marilyn Neuhart. Harry N. Abrams, 1989.

Exhibit Design: The Graphics of Trade Show Communication. Robert Konikow. PBC International, 1988.

Exhibition Design. Edited by Llorenc Bonet. Rockport, 2006.

Exhibition Design. David Dernie. W. W. Norton, 2006.

Exhibition Design. Pietro Carlo Pellegrini. teNeues, 2002.

Exhibitions in Museums. Michael Belcher. Smithsonian Books, 1993.

The Experience Economy: Work Is Theater & Every Business a Stage. B. Joseph Pine and James H. Gilmore. Harvard Business School Press, 1999.

George Nelson on Design. George Nelson. Architectural Press, 1979.

How to See: A Guide to Reading Our Man-Made Environment. George Nelson. Design Within Reach, 2003.

The Manual of Museum Exhibitions. Edited by Barry Lord and Gail Dexter Lord. AltaMira Press, 2001.

"Storytelling: The Real Work of Museums." L. Bedford. *NEMANews*, Summer 2000.

Thinking About Exhibitions. Reesa Greenberg. Routledge, 1996.

Tractatus Logico-Philosophicus. Ludwig Wittgenstein. Routledge Classics, 2001.

Trade Fair Design Annual 2001. Karin Schulte. Birkhauser, 2001.

Working with Type: Exhibitions. Rob Carter, John Demao, Sandy Wheeler, Barbara Fahs Charles, J. Tevere Macfadyen, Janice Majewski, and Mary McLaughlin. RotoVision, 2001.

World's Fairs. Erik Mattie. Princeton Architectural Press, 1998.

Magazines

Axis Magazine
www.axisinc.co.jp

AZURE
www.azuremagazine.com

bob magazine
www.bobmagazine.com

Communication Arts
www.commarts.com

DESIGN
www.design.co.kr

Domus
www.domusweb.it

EXHIBITOR Magazine
www.exhibitoronline.com

FRAME Magazine
www.framemag.com

Websites

Industrial Design Supersite
www.core77.com

National Association of Museum
Exhibition Designers
www.n-a-m-e.org

The Society for Environmental
Graphic Design
www.segd.org

Picture credits

Glossary

as-builts
Drawings created by a fabricator or designer that accurately represent the elements of an exhibition.

blockbuster
A large temporary exhibition meant to attract an audience in the hundreds of thousands or more. Blockbusters are often run by private companies and/or large institutions and generally require venues in many cities to be successful.

branded environments
Environments that are designed to promote an organization's brand, rather than as spaces for selling.

cabinets of curiosities
Private and personalized displays of objects that became a popular pursuit for wealthy European collectors in the seventeenth century.

color temperature
A characteristic of visible light that has importance in object display. The color temperature of a light source changes the apparent color of an object.

concept design
Development of the basic core story and visual design of an exhibition. All subsequent developments and designs grow out of these fundamental ideas.

conservation
The treatment, storage, and display of objects to ensure their preservation.

construction documentation
Design documentation intended to be as close to how the final exhibition will be fabricated as possible. These serve as written and drawn instructions to the fabricator and often form the basis of their contract to produce and deliver the final built and installed exhibition.

corporate exhibition
An exhibition meant to interpret and further the mission of a corporation.

demographics
An evaluation technique that studies the background and character of the exhibition audience.

design-build
Common in exhibition design, this is when the design and fabrication teams collaborate in project development from initial concept to final fabrication, often as a unified or single business entity.

design intent documentation
Drawings developed by a designer that provide general material and technical specifications for a fabricator, as well as measured drawings. They are intended for a fabricator to interpret in more detail.

donor wall
A display dedicated to the financial supporters of a building, space, or exhibition.

environmental graphics
Graphics and information meant to be viewed as part of an architectural space or outdoor environment.

exhibition design
The process or practice of developing environments that communicate a story.

exhibition narrator
A device for driving the story forward in an exhibition. Any number of media can be used as a narrator, including text, graphics, technology, or human guides. Most exhibitions employ multiple narrative media.

experience design
A business and design concept that utilizes analysis of the overall audience experience in the development of exhibition spaces.

exposition/World's Fair
Large international fairs consisting of pavilions from different countries and exhibitions built around science, technology, and culture.

focus groups
A form of evaluation that utilizes discussion groups from a small sampling of an intended exhibition audience.

formative evaluation
Testing an exhibition design concept under real-world conditions using mock-ups and prototypes.

green/sustainable design
The art of designing physical objects to comply with the principles of economic, social, and ecological sustainability. The most well-known green design concepts include recyclability, disposability, clean air and water, and energy efficiency.

heritage park
A park that contains a historic interpretive component.

house museum
An exhibition integrated into a house that interprets the stories associated with that structure.

industrial design
A design discipline that focuses on the creation of specialized objects, products, and displays.

institutional exhibition
An exhibition integrated into a government building, hospital, or school.

interactives
Mechanical, electronic, or other hands-on exhibition components that physically engage visitors with exhibition content.

LEED
Developed by the US Green Building Council, Leadership in Energy and Environmental Design (LEED) is the most well known of the rating systems developed to promote sustainability in building design.

media wall
A digital or projected display on a large scale that utilizes video or other technologies to produce dynamic, changing content.

mock-ups
Rough models of displays used to test the effectiveness of exhibition components with respect to coherence, clarity, ergonomics, etc., during the design process.

multimedia
A combination of different media used for fixed or changing content and interactive elements inside a single exhibition.

observational evaluation
A form of evaluation that includes monitoring an audience as they navigate an exhibition, followed by additional questions and surveys.

path
A physical or informational structure designed to direct the audience through an exhibition.

PDA
Personal Digital Assistant. A small digital device used to help interpret a story at a personal level in an exhibition.

proof of concept
Evaluating the strengths and weaknesses of exhibition design concepts before the further development of the design. This phase generally utilizes focus groups or behavioral analysis.

prototypes
Built segments of an exhibition that are used for testing purposes. These are the actual materials and details planned for the final components to gauge safety, durability, etc. Rapid prototyping or rapid application development techniques are used for the initial prototypes, which implement part, but not all, of the complete design.

shop drawings
Drawings developed by a fabricator that closely interpret and elaborate on those produced by the designer. These drawings detail the means, methods, materials, and technologies that will be used in the fabrication of exhibition components.

showroom
Temporary or permanent space with specially displayed items for sale.

specifications
A set of specific written instructions for the use of materials and technology in an exhibition.

standards manual
A book delivered at the end of the design process that documents the graphic and fabrication standards used in the exhibition, as well as approaches for updating content, and at times, for the maintenance of the installation.

storyboard
A series of vignettes that visually displays how the story will be conveyed in the exhibition as a series of experiences.

storytelling/narrative
The key to the development of exhibitions. All exhibitions center around a central storyline that provides an account of events or experiences.

summative evaluation
Evaluation of an exhibition after it is complete.

theater in-the-round
A circular or oblong theater where the audience is in the center and the display occurs around them, or the audience sits on the edge with the display in the center.

trade show exhibition
Trade show exhibitions are utilized to promote or sell a specific product or service, usually at a convention or exposition. These temporary exhibitions are meant to be erected and broken down quickly and displayed in large numbers inside an exhibition hall.

value engineering
A phase in the design process when an exhibition display is analyzed to reduce costs while preserving the design intent.

Index

Author biographies

Jan Lorenc

Jan Lorenc's reputation is not built on a signature style but on versatility. His team of architects, industrial designers, interior designers, and graphic designers carry out a diverse range of projects including architectural signage, exhibition and environment design, and branding. Lorenc graduated from the Illinois Institute of Technology, receiving a BS in Industrial Design and an MS in Visual Design. After working for Ted Peterson Associates, and having designed the Target logo brand, he founded Lorenc Design. He received an additional MS in Architecture at the Georgia Institute of Technology, where he met and later partnered with Chung Youl Yoo, forming Lorenc+Yoo Design. Lorenc has been named as one of the 25 monuments to environmental graphics by the Society of Environmental Graphic Design (SEGD) and has been chosen for the Advisory Board for the College of Architecture at Georgia Institute of Technology. He has received several awards, including *Print Casebooks*' "Best in Environmental Design" and "Best in Exhibition Design," as well as honors from the Institute of Design, *Graphis*, *ID Magazine*, *HOW Magazine*, *EXHIBITOR Magazine*, *Signs of the Times*, the American Institute of Graphic Arts, the American Institute of Architects, and many more.

Lee H. Skolnick

Lee H. Skolnick synthesizes art, science, and architecture to create memorable and meaningful experiences. He unlocks each project's "motivating story" to inspire imagination, curiosity, and understanding. For over 25 years, he has developed and pursued a singular approach to architecture. Based on his belief that architecture shares with other art forms the potential to embody and convey ideas and meaning by the specific means of interpretation and narrative, Skolnick has sought to unearth the unique themes and concepts which characterize each situation, and to translate them into architectural expression. Breaking down the barriers between disciplines, he has created an extraordinary firm where designers and educators work side by side. By making a thorough exploration and translation of content the starting point for design, he has brought depth, authenticity, and vision to an enormous array of projects. By applying his unique design approach to the broadest possible range of project types, Skolnick has proven the efficacy of what he calls "architecture as interpretation". He has been awarded *Architectural Digest*'s "AD100;" Cooper Union's "Achievers Under 40" and "Presidential Citation for Outstanding Achievement;" *House & Garden*'s "Design Obsession;" The Best of the Best Home Book's "House of the Year;" and local, state, and national AIA Honor Awards. Skolnick has also been elevated to the prestigious College of Fellows of the American Institute of Architects.

Craig Berger

Craig Berger is Director of Education and Professional Development for SEGD. He started as a preservation architect with John Milner Associates, before managing sign and streetscape programs for the Foundation for Architecture, where he became an expert in urban sign and interpretive programs. Since joining SEGD he has developed an educational and training program based on designer competencies and an outreach program for universities and other design associations. He has worked to expand design knowledge through an extensive educational program of workshops, lectures, teleconferences, and publications in three areas: wayfinding, information design, and exhibition design. He has also developed a program to spearhead the placement of environmental graphic design and exhibition design programs in universities, in the process of which he taught wayfinding design at Florida International University, Iowa State University, and Kent State University. He is also developing exhibition design programs at the University of Leicester and the Fashion Institute of Technology. He is currently leading a testing and educational program on a set of universal healthcare symbols on behalf of Hablamos Juntos with the Robert Wood Johnson Foundation. Berger has a BA and a bachelor's of architecture from Pennsylvania State University, and a Master's of Business Administration from Temple University. He is the author of RotoVision's *Wayfinding*.